All-Around-the-House
ART *and* CRAFT *Book*

All-Around-the-House ART *and* CRAFT *Book*

by Patricia Z. Wirtenberg

Photographs by Patricia Z. Wirtenberg

1968 HOUGHTON MIFFLIN COMPANY BOSTON

Lovingly to Mom and Dad . . . and, especially, to my husband who envisioned, encouraged, and enjoyed. Life, with Lee, is *good*.

CONTENTS

PREFACE

LEARNING to create works of art from materials in your own house can be both inexpensive and fun for you. A young person of any age can do it, and it doesn't have to be a complicated, expensive or formal process. It can be easygoing, eye-opening and taste-expanding as you begin to see old things in a new light, as you begin to arrange and relate ordinary things in an extraordinary way. You'll understand form when you begin to work with the unnoticed shape of a detergent bottle or a vegetable container. You'll feel texture when you touch wood and wool with a new awareness. Colors will come alive when you search for them in foodstuffs and fallen leaves.

Just look around you! That's the first and most important step in creating an artist's environment for yourself. You don't need a country barn or a garret with a skylight. You don't need oil paints and canvas. Imagination, ideas, a searching attitude and the materials of ordinary life — those are the things that an artist really works with. In *The All-Around-the-House Art Book*, those are the things that you will work with.

The projects in this book have been designed to help you to explore your way into the artist's world, to experiment with the materials you find and to enjoy the fun and excitement of creating art all-around-the-house. You don't need to buy any special artists' materials; almost everything you need is already somewhere near you.

So look around the home you live in, whether it is a three-story house, or a three-room apartment. Look into your attic (in an apartment, your "attic" may be a storage chest or a catch-all upper shelf in a closet). Look into the garage, the kitchen, the laundry and the backyard.

From whatever you find — old newspapers, chicken bones, shoe polish, egg cartons, soap powders, fabrics, hangers and starch — you'll make paintings, collages, mosaics, prints and sculpture.

And in this process of trying, experimenting and doing, you'll discover the joy of creating art with materials that are all-around-the-house.

All-Around-the-House

ART *and* CRAFT *Book*

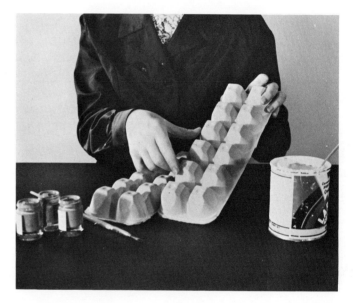

PAINTED EGG CARTONS

a study of color arrangement in three dimensions

LOOK AT ANY egg carton. Study a single section for holding one egg and you will see that it has eight or more sides. If you then count the connecting areas of the carton between the individual egg cup sections, you will see that the carton is an interesting arrangement of many separate surfaces.

If you were planning to design such an arrangement of surfaces and found an interesting pattern was already available to you in the form of an egg carton, your "work" is half done!

The idea of this project is to create a visual arrangement by painting each surface a separate color. The colors that are next to one another must be related and, with so many sides to paint, it takes planning to see that two side-by-side areas don't end up with the same color. You'll discover that the painting step itself is not very difficult, but the planning of where the colors go, before you begin to paint, takes time.

You'll need three or more colors for painting. These few colors can then be mixed to give you many more

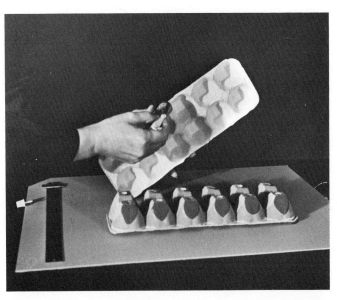

colors. You'll also need glue and a flat piece of cardboard if you wish to mount your finished painted egg carton. (I prefer to work on two egg cartons at one time for it makes my finished piece larger and more important.)

If you begin to paint by choosing one color and painting the same side of all the egg sections this color, your work will go smoothly. Once the first color is painted, wash your brush and go on with the second color. Keep changing colors until all the sides and connecting areas are painted.

The paint will dry quickly on the absorbent cardboard material of the egg carton. When each carton is dry you can then glue it onto a large sheet of cardboard.

The colors you have chosen and the design you have made by your arrangement of those colors on the many surfaces of the carton will give it a "personality" of its own. Is it gay or is it serious? Is it loud or quiet? Try painting more cartons using other color schemes to create an entirely different egg carton "personality"!

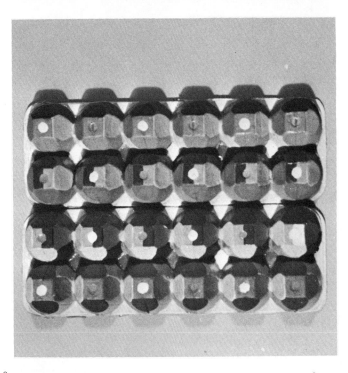

3

CUBE ART

transforming sugar cubes with paint

FOR THIS PROJECT you will need a box of notched sugar cubes, thick poster paints (or house paints) in three or four colors, gold or silver paint, fast-drying glue, a sheet of plywood or *very* stiff cardboard for the background, and some sandpaper.

To begin, snap dozens of sugar cubes in half at the notch. Mix the three or four starting colors in various combinations with each other so that you have many more colors. Such mixing always produces colors that are harmoniously related to one another.

Paint the sides of each cube a color and then paint its top a contrasting color. Try as many side and top combinations as you can imagine. Leave the bottom side of the cube unpainted; it will be later glued to the background. You may want to paint a few cubes all gold or all silver. These metal-colored cubes will add a "sparkle" to your finished wall relief.

When the paint has dried, you can begin to assemble your creation. First of all, measure and mark the center of your background. Start your Cube Art at this point and work from the center out toward both sides and toward the top and bottom. Leave a wide border on all

four sides, with the bottom border being slightly wider than the other three. This will be your frame area.

The sugar cubes are glued on in horizontal and vertical rows. Glue some of the unpainted bottom sides flat against the background, but glue the others at angles so that their painted sides show. Occasionally you will need to sandpaper a corner to glue the angled cubes firmly to the board. The more irregular the surface is the more interesting it will be. Light will catch on this bumpy surface and it will be far more beautiful than if all the pieces are applied flat.

While you are in the process of gluing, you must also remember that you are composing a pleasing color design. Isn't it more interesting if you avoid the ordinary pattern of a checkerboard which puts light colors next to dark colors? Instead, similar colors can be grouped together. You can also insert a gold or silver cube here and there for added variety. End your gluing with edges that are straight on all four sides. This border will frame your finished Cube Art. Select one of your darkest colors and paint the frame area.

Once you have mastered the technique, you may want to experiment with a circular or diagonal arrangement of cubes.

VEGETABLE PRINTING

printing with fruits and vegetables

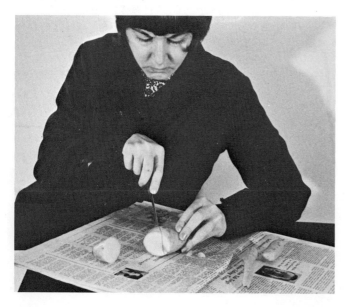

THERE ARE NUMEROUS ways of making prints, some more complicated or expensive than others. Vegetable Printing is one of the simplest, best-known and least expensive of all printing methods.

You can use any hard vegetable or fruit such as a potato, turnip, carrot, apple, radish, onion or pear. You'll also need a knife, some scrap paper for experimenting and some better paper for printing. The printing "ink" is poster paint.

Begin by cutting your fruit or vegetable into slices or wedges of varying sizes—large or small, thick or thin. Then use your knife to dig out a simple design on the face of the slice. You might even try notching or scalloping its edges. You can design or decorate the vegetable slice a lot or a little. You may want to leave a slice or two plain and undecorated if you like its shape just the way it is.

When you have a few pieces ready, you can start printing. Select one interesting slice and apply paint to the face of it, keeping the paint fairly thick. First, press your slice to scrap paper. Lift it without wiggling it on the paper. Remember that printing is an up-and-down motion. If you push or drag your vegetable, you'll blur the color and smear the print. When you want to change colors, either use another piece of vegetable or wash the one that you are using.

Try some different effects: mix two colors directly on the slice by painting one half one color and the other half another color; use the edges of very thin slices to print; try printing one shape over another and one color over another.

When you've experimented enough on scrap paper, try printing on a better piece of paper. You can print an abstract design or you can print a realistic picture. It's up to you!

TINFOIL ENGRAVING

a way of denting a smooth surface

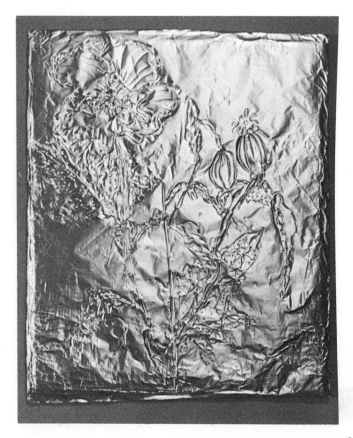

THE IDEA OF TINFOIL ENGRAVING is to draw on the foil with a pointed tool which is sharp enough to dent the surface of the foil but dull or rounded enough not to cut through it.

The materials you will need are tinfoil, a stiff piece of cardboard, some newspaper, cellophane tape and some "engraving" tools such as a knitting needle, a large nail or the handle end of a spoon.

Tear or cut several sheets of newspaper to the size of the piece of cardboard. Tear off a large sheet of tinfoil so that when it is doubled, it will be larger than the cardboard by several inches. Double the foil and place it on top of the pad of newspaper. Doubling the foil and cushioning it underneath with newspaper will help to prevent your tool from cutting through the foil. Secure the foil in place by wrapping the edges behind the cardboard and taping them to the back. Smooth out any wrinkles with your hands. The tinfoil surface is now ready for engraving.

Draw your picture with your tool directly onto the foil. Work carefully, for lines once engraved cannot be easily "erased." Experiment with lines made by different tools. A knitting needle makes a line entirely different from that made by a key or your fingernail.

Try to draw with long, connected strokes for short broken lines look ragged and unsure. Use finer tools for finer details after using more blunt, broader tools for large outlines.

When you frame your Tinfoil Engraving, be careful not to press down on the face of the engraving as you fit the frame or the engraved lines will be flattened and their detail dulled.

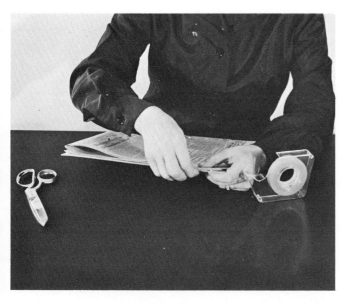

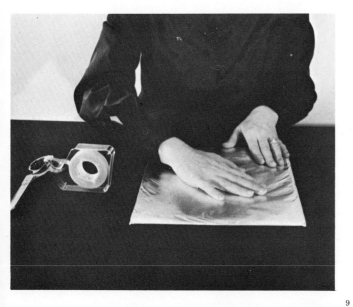

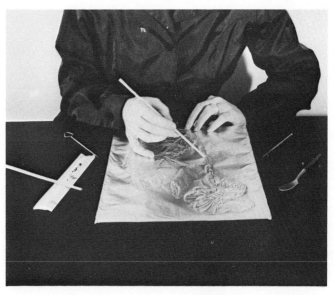

CALCIUM COLLAGE

a picture made from bones and shells

THIS AMUSING COLLAGE starts from one special kind of leftover. Of course, you'll have to rescue this art material before any one else disposes of it as "garbage." The leftovers can be poultry or meat bones and crab, clam, oyster or lobster shells. You can even include eggshells. You'll also need a stiff background in a dark, rich color and some fast-drying glue.

Bones will be found in many shapes. They can be small, medium or large, thick or thin. Shells are even more varied in size and shape. They will probably add more color to your collage than bones, especially if they include the red-orange of boiled lobster and crab shells.

First, wash and dry all your materials thoroughly. Seashells should be washed in soapy water to rid them of their fishy odor. Bones can be dried in the air or in an oven.

Start your picture by placing some bones and shells on your background and then experiment with different arrangements. This arranging and rearranging is very important, for you are letting the materials themselves suggest the idea and the composition of your picture. That's exactly the way many contemporary artists work.

When you've arranged a picture that pleases you,

you can start to glue the pieces onto the background. Pick up each bone or shell, one by one, and apply glue to its edge. Place it back into the composition.

Don't limit yourself to working with whole pieces of shells. You can crush eggshells and small clam shells to make a material which is particularly suited for filling in odd-shaped areas and creating a gravel-like texture. Also, consider using the glossy, pearly inside of mussel or oyster shells in some part of your picture.

Don't worry if other people call you a garbage collector. Remember that most artists are usually misunderstood.

VEGETARIAN MOSAICS

a unique collage using a mosaic technique

THIS PROJECT is one of the most exciting to do, for you'll be learning an unusual technique besides adventuring with texture and color. Ordinary mosaics are made from clay or glass tiles, called tesserae. In making Vegetarian Mosaics, however, *foodstuffs* and *spices* take the place of the tiles.

You will need these basic materials to begin: a piece of plywood for the background, or a *very* stiff piece of cardboard; white liquid glue; a pad of newspaper and clear lacquer for the final step of preserving your mosaic.

It would be impossible to list all the foodstuffs and spices that can be used to make a Vegetarian Mosaic, for such a list would run into hundreds items. Your Vegetarian Mosaic will depend on what is available from your mother's kitchen or in nearby markets. The following is a partial listing of foodstuffs that I have

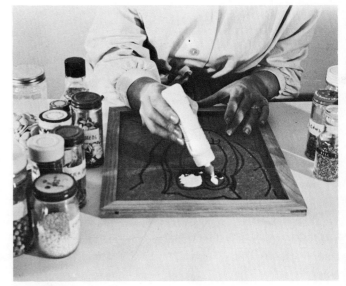

tried and found work well: pea, lima, fava, turtle, mung, kidney, pinto and coffee beans; tea, rosemary, laurel, oregano and mint leaves; curry, mustard and garlic powders; salt; pepper; instant and ground coffee; sesame, cumin, coriander, dill and poppy seeds; dried corn, peas and okra, rice; barley; cereals and many types of macaroni.

The first step is to draw your subject on the plywood background. If possible, put a frame on the plywood at this starting point. The frame acts as a "retaining wall" during the making of your Vegetarian Mosaic; it helps to keep the glue and foodstuffs in place. Study your available supply of tesserae, namely, the foodstuffs, deciding what material will be used for what area. Plan you mosaic for contrasts of color, texture and size of materials. I try to avoid outlining my subject with

dark or light beans for this can make a hard and unattractive line.

Squeeze out enough glue to cover a small area of your subject. Select a foodstuff, perhaps kidney beans, and place it into the glue, fitting them carefully next to one another. Then work another area, applying more glue and filling that area with the chosen foodstuff.

You will notice that, before it dries, the white glue shows *between* pieces of foodstuff, such as between the beans. When this small area dries, the glue shows as an unattractive blank spot. Therefore, all such in-between areas must also be filled in by sprinkling a fine seed or powder, such as poppy or curry, over the *entire* large area in which the small spaces that exist. Press this fine material into the glue with your hand. The "fill" will

stay only where the glue is. When you wish to remove the excess material, lift the panel upright *quickly* and shake the "fill" onto a pad of newspaper. Since the glue is still wet, you must work very fast as you tip the panel or the glue and foodstuffs will slide from the plywood. Any excess materials collected on the newspaper can be poured into a bottle or box for later reuse. Continue to squeeze glue, place materials, fill in and remove excesses until the mosaic is completed, with the *exception* of the background.

For the background, choose your material carefully. You need a foodstuff that will be good for covering a large area and one that will, at the same time, contrast well with the materials used for your subject. I have found that products such as salt, poppy seed, ground

coffee or tea leaves are excellent for filling in large areas. Coat the entire background with glue, shake on the selected material and press it well into the glue. Allow your mosaic to dry for several hours or overnight before removing the excess of this last foodstuff.

Although a Vegetarian Mosaic will last a long time without a protective coat of lacquer, it is preferable to try to "seal" it against the ravages of time and insects. To do this, you must first allow your completed mosaic to dry out for a full week. Then apply two generous coats (allow drying time between coats) of clear lacquer. You'll be amazed to see how the lacquer brightens up the colors of the foodstuffs and, at the same time, adds the protection needed to insure a mosaic of long-lasting quality.

15

PLASTIC CUP CUT-UP

a wall hanging assembled from plastic rings

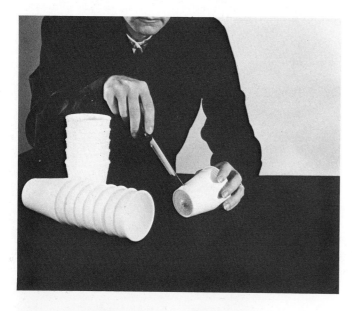

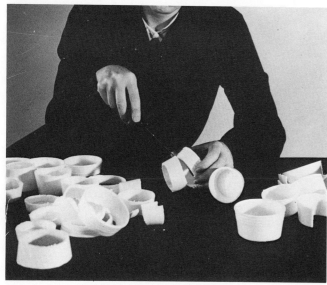

THIS DECORATIVE WALL HANGING is made by assembling slices cut from thermal beverage cups.

In this project you'll use the kind of thick-walled plastic hot beverage cup which is made from Styrofoam. You can substitute another type of cup, but the final result will differ from the sculpture illustrated in the photographs. This Styrofoam cup is usually sold bagged in large quantities and is quite inexpensive. You will also need sandpaper, rubber cement, a knife and metallic spray paint for the cups.

Begin by slicing ten to fourteen cups into rings, using an ordinary table knife. Vary the width of the rings from ½″ to 2″. Cut across some of the rings to produce half circles. If the edges of the slices are rough from cutting, smooth them with sandpaper.

Spread out all the pieces in front of you. Play with different combinations and groupings of shapes. Try nestling pieces within pieces. Place some rings at angles to one another. Add some of the solid-bottom circles, from the bottoms of the cups, here and there. Assemble small groups first, rather than trying to put together one large piece of sculpture. Later on, these small groups will be permanently connected into a single arrangement.

Rubber cement is one of the best glues to adhere the rings together. Other glues may dissolve the plastic material. When you are ready to glue, it is not necessary to take your groupings apart. Simply separate two touching pieces, brush on some rubber cement and press the two pieces back together as they were.

After experimenting with several arrangements, glue the smaller groups together to form the final large shape.

Allow the rubber cement to dry thoroughly. Your wall hanging can then be spray-painted to change it from its original white color. I like to use paint in metallic colors to give this feather-light plastic wall hanging the appearance of heavy brass or silver sculpture.

STRAW CONSTRUCTIONS

an assemblage of drinking straws

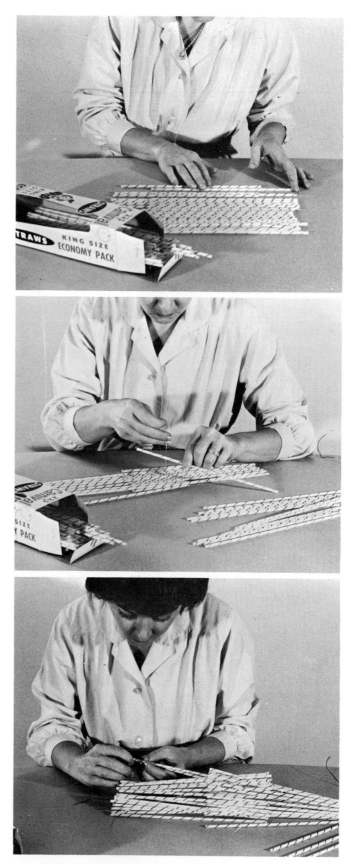

THIS PROJECT shows you how to string dozens of straws together to make a complex yet trim and linear construction.

The materials needed are a large box of paper straws either plain, patterned or transparent; a block of Styrofoam for the base; a slim dowel about two feet long and some very fine wire. (If you wish to paint your finished piece, you'll need spray paint in one or two colors. I like to use black plus a metal color.)

Snip a length of fine wire about 18″ long. If you can put this wire on a large needle, the threading will go quite quickly. Otherwise, you may find it necessary to puncture with a pin two tiny holes in each straw, about 1/3 the distance from one end, and then push the wire through. Thread this wire through one straw at a time.

Repeat this process until about forty to fifty straws have been threaded onto the wire. Stretch the wire out on your table, with the straws threaded onto it. Flip over every other straw so that half the straws have their long part on the left side of the wire and the other have their long part on the right side of the wire.

Now cut two shorter lengths of wire, about 7″ each. Using the same method, thread one of these wires through the loose ends of the straws on the left side and the other wire through the loose ends of the straws on the right side. Form a circle out of each of the three wires by twisting their ends together. When you do this the straws will take the shape of interlocking cones. You can help the shaping by spreading out the straws along the wire circles so that they are evenly spaced. This completes one section.

Assemble three or more of these sections. When you have done this, set the dowel upright into the Styrofoam base. This slender dowel (though nearly invisible in the finished piece) acts as the central support for the construction. Lower the first section onto the dowel so that the dowel passes between some straws but comes out through one of the smaller closed-circle ends. Lower a second section onto the dowel so that it is at any angle to the first section. When the straws on two sections meet, they will interlock with one another. Add the remaining sections by this threading-on and interlocking method.

Unless you've used colorful, transparent cellophane straws, you'll probably want to change the color of your finished construction. This is easily done with spray paint.

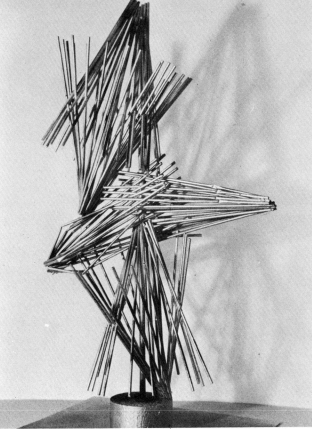

KITCHEN CLAY

a modeling material made on the stove

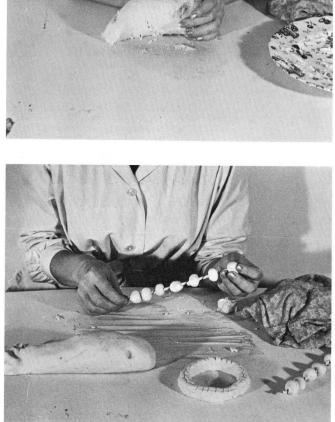

AN EXCELLENT, inexpensive modeling material can be made from a simple formula using a few ingredients from the kitchen. Kitchen Clay hardens without baking, and it can be easily modeled and then painted. The ingredients needed are baking soda, cornstarch and water.

Here's the "recipe": combine 4 cups of baking soda, 2 cups of cornstarch and 2½ cups of water in a saucepan. Warm this mixture over moderate heat, stirring constantly. When the mixture thickens to a dough-like consistency, turn it out onto a dish or sheet of tinfoil. When it is cool enough to handle, knead it for two or three minutes until it feels smooth.

Always cover Kitchen Clay with a damp cloth to keep it soft. If you want to keep it soft overnight, place it in a plastic bag and seal the bag tightly.

Kitchen Clay is modeled like any ordinary clay. It can be squeezed, rolled or pinched. You can make jewelry or you can make sculpture with it. You will find, however, that very large pieces develop cracks as they dry, so it is better to keep your pieces no larger than a big banana.

Perhaps you would like to make someone a string of beads for a present? To make a Kitchen Clay necklace roll out about twenty or thirty small balls. Thread these balls onto a few paper straws. The straws make a

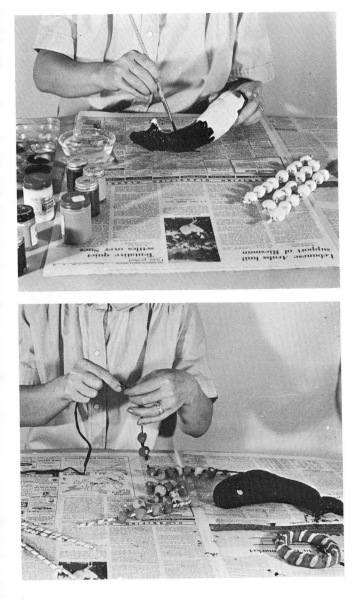

hole for stringing and also serve as a good holder for the beads while they harden and while they are being painted.

A bracelet can be made from the same kind of beads or, more simply, from a string of clay with its ends pinched together to form a circle.

You can even decorate the surface of the clay on whatever object you model by using any tool, flat or pointed. For example, a pencil point can be used to dent an interesting decoration into the soft clay.

Kitchen Clay will air-harden in one or two days. If the drying must be hurried, you can put your pieces in an oven which has been set at its lowest temperature for about three hours.

The dried clay is fairly hard and durable. It takes any kind of paint well, from poster to house paint. If you finish your poster-painted pieces with a coat of lacquer, this will enhance the colors, especially on painted beads.

To string your necklace, find a long length of heavy yarn or a shoelace. Tie the first bead at one end of this strand. Then tie a knot after this bead and add a second bead. Tie another knot. The beads are strung so that a knot always separates them. This knotting method uses fewer beads and makes the necklace lighter. End the stringing with a loop just large enough to pass over the first bead so that the ends of your necklace are connected.

'GATOR SCULPTURE

food cartons become an animal sculpture

In today's supermarkets, fruits, vegetables and eggs come packaged in sturdy and colorful cartons which stimulate the imagination. Their odd shapes suggest subjects far from their original purpose.

This 'Gator Sculpture uses a few egg cartons, three rectangular-shaped cartons, some large pieces of stiff cardboard, colored tissue paper, glue or staples, paint and scissors.

First of all, draw an outline of a large alligator, about three feet long, from its neck to its tail, on heavy cardboard. Omit the head for now because that's constructed later. Cut out this outline. Then draw and cut out two pairs of legs from another piece of cardboard. Be sure to make the rear legs longer and fatter than the front ones, because that's the way an alligator is built.

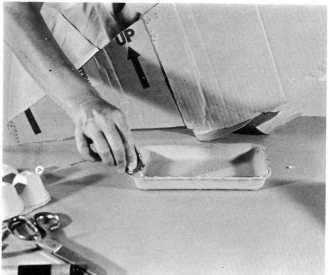

Attach the legs by gluing or stapling them into place on the body shape. Glue or staple the body shape over a rectangular carton. This carton shapes the 'Gator's belly and lifts your sculpture off the ground to give it a more natural look. Now bend the legs so that they touch the ground.

Glue several egg cartons to the back of the alligator, cutting and tapering them whenever necessary to fit the shape of the body. Be sure that some of the egg cups extend into the tail section.

To construct the head, staple or glue two same-sized rectangular cartons together at one end giving the appearance of gaping jaws. Taper the cartons and notch their edges to resemble snapping jaws with mean, jagged teeth.

Line the bottom and the roof of the 'Gator's mouth with crumpled, bright-pink tissue paper. Add halves of eggshells for its bulging eyes.

Join the head securely to the body by stapling or gluing these parts together.

Study a nature book in order to paint your 'Gator in a realistic way with green, black and brown. Use spray paint, if you can, for this will be easy. If you'd prefer to make a "fun" 'Gator, paint him in stripes, polka dots or checks!

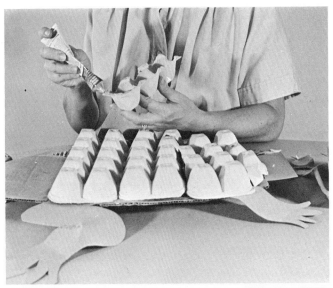

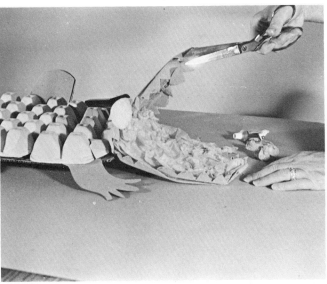

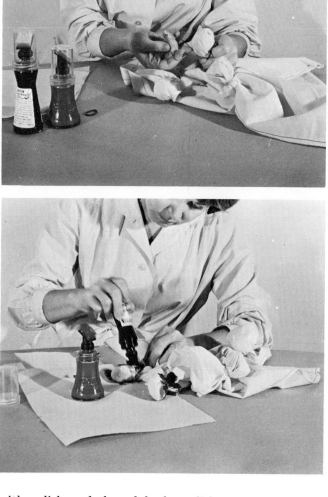

SHOE POLISH BANNER

tie-dyeing brought up to date

THIS PROJECT modernizes and simplifies a Victorian craft of fabric dyeing by using some of today's time-saving products. "Tie-dyeing" is the name given to this old yet new method of creating a design on fabric by bundling and tying the material so that the dye cannot by absorbed by all parts equally.

The materials needed to create your tie-dye banner are a large piece of white or pastel-colored cloth such as sheeting, elastic bands, paper towels, liquid shoe polish in 2 or more colors and 2 narrow dowels. Before actually dyeing, turn and stitch any ragged edges of your sheeting to give it "finished" look.

Begin by crumpling up a sheet of paper towel into a ball. Slip this ball under a part of the cloth and make a small lump by twisting the cloth around the paper ball. Hold the lump in place with a tight elastic band. Repeat this procedure, making many lumps scattered in a random pattern over the entire piece of cloth. However, be sure that the lumps are at least 6" apart.

Select one color of shoe polish. Wet the applicator with polish and then dab the polish onto each of the lumps. Also apply the polish above and below the elastic bands. Don't try to drown the fabric with polish but let it go only where it flows by light dabbing. Change to a second color of polish and add touches of this color to the already-colored lumps.

Release all the elastic bands and discard the polish-stained wads of paper. Study the "accidental" design that you've made. Does your banner need more color? Is it patterned enough?

To complete the banner, tie some new lumps in un-dyed areas or overlap them with already-dyed spots. Experiment with different kinds of strokes and different amounts of polish. Release the bands once again and study your results. You'll probably agree that after

two tyings your banner has a richer, more satisfactory pattern.

When you have finished tying and dyeing, your banner will be quite wrinkled and in need of a pressing. After it has dried thoroughly, spread the banner flat on a thick pad of newspaper and iron it lightly with a medium-warm iron. You can expect that a little color will run from the cloth onto the paper.

Hang your banner by mounting it on the dowels. One dowel is placed along the top edge and the banner is glued or stapled to it. Tie on a length of cord or yarn across this dowel so that you can hang your banner. The second dowel, fastened to the bottom edge will weight the banner down. If a dowel isn't available any other straight sticks will do nearly as well.

"TAKE-AWAY" BLEACH PICTURES

a reverse painting venture

THE AIM OF THIS PROJECT is to *subtract* color rather than to add it. As a matter of fact, the color will disappear almost as fast as you "paint"! The materials needed are colored construction paper, a cupful of liquid bleach and a spoon, old brush, or paper straw for spreading the bleach.

Select a brightly-colored piece of construction paper, placing it in front of you on the table. Scoop up a little bleach with a spoon or on a brush. Drop the bleach

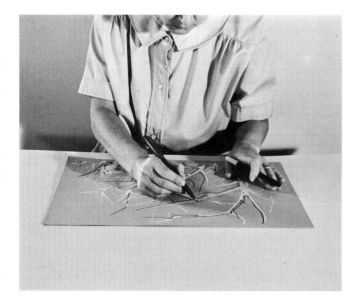

onto your colored paper and *immediately* spread the blob around by brushing it or pushing it out with the spoon. Be careful of your clothes, because the color will fade them just as quickly as the paper.

For fun you can use a paper straw to blow at the drops of bleach. The force of your blowing will scatter the bleach in all directions, making long, fine lines. Within seconds, you will see the colored paper begin to fade and, in less than a minute, *all* the original color of the paper wet by the bleach will *disappear*. Delicate feathery lines, which look like twigs and grass, result from this technique.

If you've started with a fairly dark paper, the light, bleached lines will contrast sharply with it. If, however, your paper was of a lighter tone, you may want to add some dark, drawn lines for accent. Use ordinary crayons or a laundry marking pen to accent here and there.

DIP AND DAB

textured pictures printed with sponges

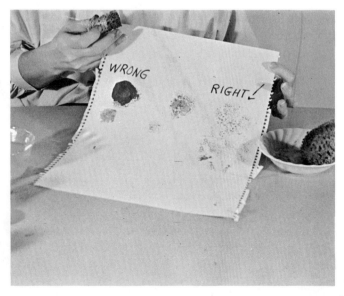

Look around the laundry for some sponges. You'll discover that sponges come in two types. Natural sponges which come from the ocean look rough with their large, irregular holes. Man-made sponges are usually smooth and regularly-shaped.

For materials you'll need a few pieces of sponge (either natural, man-made or both), poster paints, a jar of water, a shallow dish, scrap paper and paper for printing.

Pour a little paint into your dish. Dampen your sponge in water and squeeze it out well. Dip your sponge lightly into the paint. Dab the sponge on scrap paper until you can clearly see a print of the texture of your sponge. This texture print should have "holes" in it, somewhat like Swiss cheese. The holes will be either large or small depending on the type of sponge you are using.

Without dipping into the paint again, dab the sponge onto your good paper, making a clear print. Remember that printing is an up-and-down motion. Dragging your sponge will smear the print and make it fuzzy rather than crisp and clean.

When changing colors, rinse your sponge in clear water or use a separate piece of sponge for each color. If you print one color over another, be sure that the paint of the first print has dried or the colors will run together. "Draw" your picture. Build it sponge-print by sponge-print. If your picture needs some details or outlines, draw some lines with a laundry marking pen or with crayons.

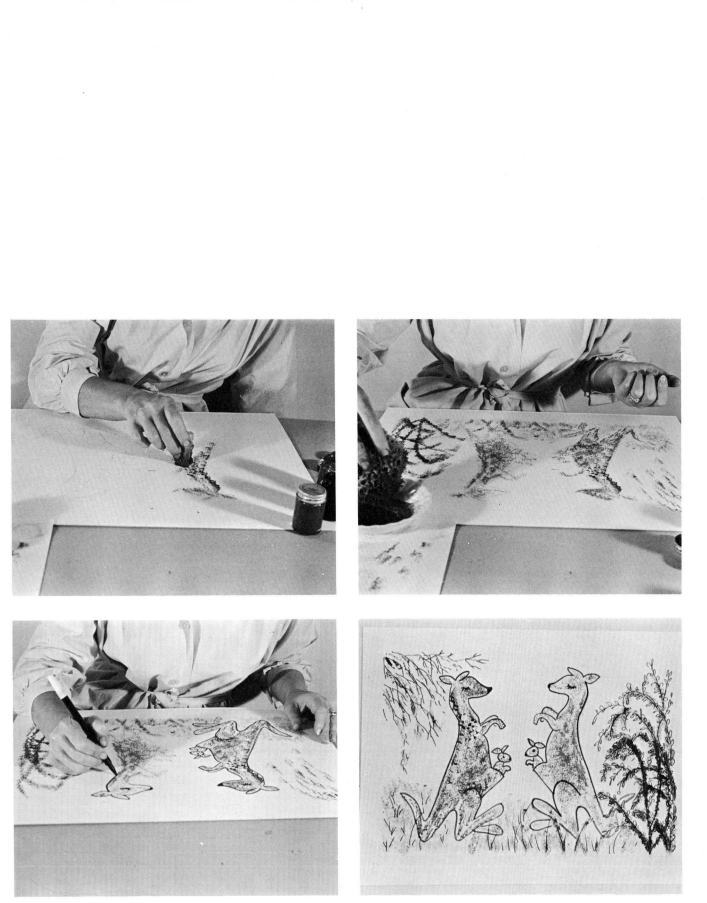

SOAP POWDER PICTURES

"printing" in relief

THIS PROJECT resembles a kind of "printing" although the method is rather unusual. A Soap Powder Picture starts with a piece of paper on which lines are "drawn" with a tube of glue. These wet glue lines are pressed into mounds of soap powder. When the different colored powders stick to the glue, the lines become visible and your picture emerges.

The materials needed are colored construction paper or ordinary cardboard, a tube of fast-drying glue, soap powder in one or two colors and a pencil.

If you investigate the housecleaning section of any supermarket, you'll find that laundry powders come in several colors in addition to the common white. Some powders are manufactured with green or blue dots scattered in the white powder, while other powders are all blue or all green. It's possible to "print" with a single color of powder, but your picture will be prettier if you can use two or three colors.

Pour out a small mound of each soap powder. Choose a background paper that contrasts with your soap powders. Sketch your subject on this background paper with a light pencil. Then retrace the lines with glue in a small section no more than a few inches wide. While the glue is still wet, flip your paper over quickly and press the glue into one of the soap powders. Lift the paper and tap it gently in order to remove the excess soap powder. The soap will stick only where there is glue. Continue to "print" your picture, section by section.

Colors are changed easily by dipping the wet glue lines into one color or another of soap powder. When the glue has dried, the raised-powder areas will be quite firm and hard.

Don't let your picture get wet. A Soap Powder Picture turns into a soap suds picture very easily!

YARN AND STARCH PICTURES

collages made without paste

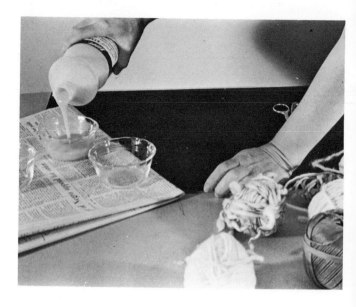

"Collage" is the name given to artwork which is pasted or glued together. In this project, however, liquid starch takes the place of the "paste" and the pictures are "drawn" with yarn.

The materials you'll need are some small bowls, scissors, liquid starch, pieces of yarn and string and a stiff colored background. Your collage will be more attractive if you can find yarns of different colors and thicknesses, from fine fingering yarn to bulky rug yarn.

Pour a little liquid starch into the bowls. Snip some pieces of yarn into strands about 12″ or so. Soak these strands in starch, separating the white yarn from the colored yarn in case some dye runs. Let the yarn absorb the starch for a few minutes. Then lift out a single strand. Remove the excess starch by running your fingers gently down the strand, allowing the excess starch to run back into the bowl. The yarn should look "wet," but starch should not be seen dripping from it.

Touch one end of a wet strand to your background paper, and with your fingers as guides, "draw" with the yarn as you drop it into place. Combine different colors and types of yarn as you "draw" your picture. Also, your collage will be more effective if you outline some areas and fill in other areas solidly.

It is difficult to keep your background clean and free from starch drips, no matter how carefully and neatly you work. A good many starch blobs can be avoided by not working with overly-wet strands of yarn and, of course, by not shifting any strands from one place to another, once it is part of your background.

When your Yarn and Starch Picture is finished, place it on some flat surface until it dries. Since its corners will tend to curl up a little as it dries, they must be weighted down without flattening any part of your picture.

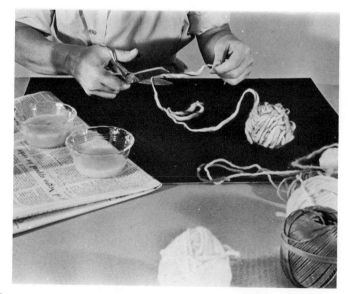

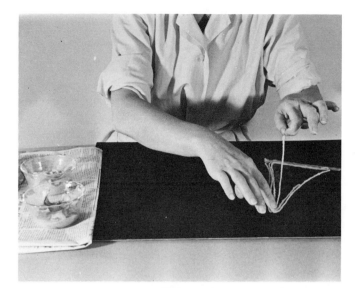

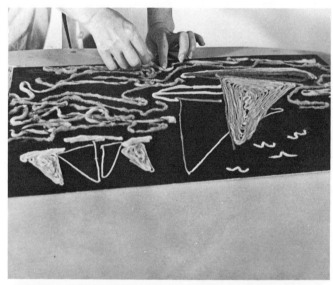

"TOUCH-ME" PLAQUES

a high-relief collage

"TOUCH-ME" Plaques are collages made from ordinary cheesecloth and liquid starch. Their highly-raised surfaces invite your fingers to trace the designs and feel the texture. For materials you'll need cheesecloth, liquid starch, scissors, a bowl, stiff cardboard for a background and poster or spray paints.

Begin by cutting some cheesecloth into twenty or more strips about 1″–2″ wide. Soak these strips in a bowl of liquid starch. Cut another piece of cheesecloth which is large enough to cover and wrap around your piece of cardboard. Dip this large piece of cheesecloth into starch and apply it directly to one side of the cardboard. Smooth the cloth until it is wrinkle-free and then turn the edges around to the back. Once the background is covered with cheesecloth, you can begin to shape your plaque.

With your subject in mind, place a strip of starch-soaked cheesecloth on the background and pull, push or pile it into the proper shape and position. Use your fingers to build up raised, rather than flattened, lines with the strips of cheesecloth.

Continue to build your plaque in this way, adding starch-soaked strips one by one, until it is completed. Then allow the plaque to dry overnight.

As it dries, the cardboard will probably begin to curl up in the corners. You can avoid this unpleasant happening by weighting the plaque down on all four corners while it is still wet. Be careful not to flatten any of its raised part as you apply the weights.

You'll notice that your dried plaque has taken on a faint blue cast—the color of the liquid starch. If you like this effect, you can consider your project finished. If you prefer to brighten the plaque you can paint it with poster paints or spray-paint it. Try adding a touch of gold or silver paint here and there for an interesting highlight.

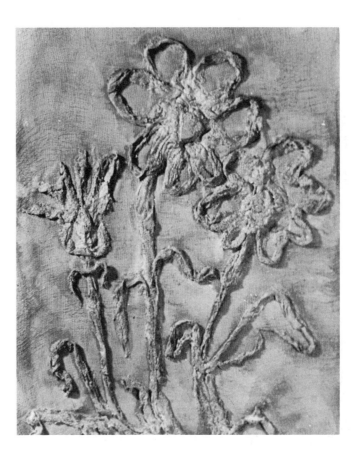

POPPING OUT PLASTER PARTS

casting in plastic molds

MANY LAUNDRY PRODUCTS (soap, bleach, starch, softener, detergent) come in plastic containers which have unique and interesting shapes. In this project, you will pour a mixture into several of these plastic containers to create plaster pieces which will later be combined into a single, exciting assemblage.

For materials you'll need several plastic containers in various shapes and sizes, sandpaper, water and plaster of paris. Begin by studying the shapes of your plastic containers. Since the container is your mold for future plaster shapes, you can fill it to any height that will give you a beautifully-cast shape. Can you get a better shape filling it partway or all the way to the top? It's up to you to decide how much plaster to pour into each container.

When you are ready to pour, mix the plaster according to directions but add more water than called for. A more liquid mixture takes longer to harden, and therefore, it will not begin to "set up" while you are in the midst of the delicate operation of pouring plaster into many molds! Fill at least five containers with plaster to the height you desire. A funnel will come in handy if you are guiding plaster into narrow-necked containers.

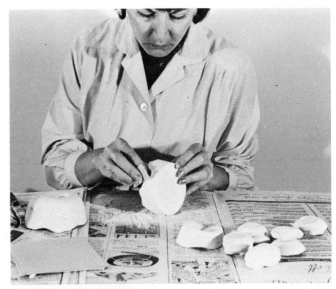

Leave the plaster in the molds until it dries. Then, free the plaster shapes from the molds. Usually, the shapes can be removed easily by "popping" them out as if they were ice cubes being released from a tray. However, if the shape of the mold is such that it imprisons your plaster piece, you must slit it open to release the casting.

When the shapes are removed from the molds, some of their edges might need sandpapering to smooth them out. If you like the white color of plaster, it is not necessary to paint your work. Otherwise, you can tone the shapes with almost any kind of paint, stain or varnish.

Place all the cast shapes before you on a table. Study them to see how they differ from one another. Begin to stack some shapes, experimenting with different arrangements. Your assemblage will be most effective if you do not pile up the shapes tightly, like bricks in a wall. Try some shapes at angles to one another. Overlap or overhang other pieces. Your assemblage is finished when the shapes you have grouped together please you. If you wish to keep this composition together permanently, you can attach touching pieces with a strong glue.

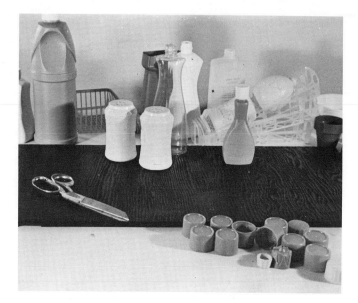

PLASTIC MAIDEN

a colorful, 3-dimensional plastic assemblage

TODAY many of our necessary and useful household products come in bottles, boxes and other containers formed from molded plastic. And the colors used in these containers are like a rainbow, from red to lavender! You can find blue, green, red, aqua, white and purple bottles holding laundry products, plus pink, yellow or turquoise containing scouring products. In the kitchen you'll find citrus juices dispensed in lemon and lime containers. Even the bottle caps are apt to be some bright color like orange or magenta. Once you've begun to search and collect these items, you'll be amazed at the variety of colors to be found.

The materials you'll need for the Plastic Maiden are plastic containers in many sizes, shapes and colors, a stiff background painted a dark color, scissors and glue.

Spread out your collection of plastic pieces and begin to arrange them on your background. Move the pieces around until they suggest the idea for your plastic assemblage. When you have your idea, you'll probably want to cut and shape some of the whole, rounded containers so that their edges will lie flat, for gluing, against the background. The cutting of plastic may be easy or difficult, depending on the thickness of that particular container. Avoid the tops and bottoms of bottles because they are molded from a double thickness of plastic and are nearly impossible to cut.

When you are completely satisfied with your arrangement of plastic pieces, you can begin to glue them permanently to your background. Lift each piece, one by one, and squeeze glue along its edges. Replace the piece into your assemblage. Experiment with different effects such as gluing plastic on top of plastic or clear plastic over colored plastic.

Your friends will enjoy trying to identify the products which gave you all the pretty colors in your assemblage.

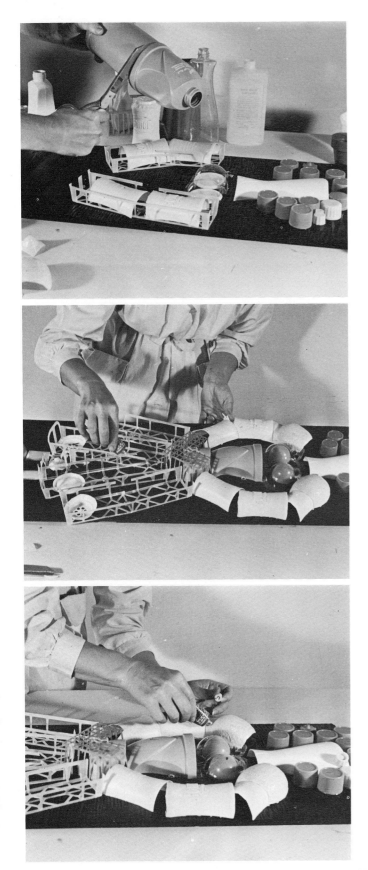

HANGER SCULPTURE

bending wire clothes hangers into new forms

No MATTER how often you sort through your closets, almost every home ends up with too many wire clothes hangers. Here's an idea that uses up those extra hangers by bending them and combining them to make a piece of sculpture. This project is planned so that your hangers can be shaped by bending them, rather than requiring you to cut them into pieces, for cutting wire hangers is a difficult task.

The materials you'll need are 15–20 wire hangers, adhesive tape, liquid starch, paper towels, string and spray paints in one or two colors.

First, bend all your hangers in this way: hold a single hanger so that you are grasping the ends with both hands. Fold these ends toward each other so that they are then an inch or so apart. Bend the curved hanging hook so that it tips down to one side or the other. Shape half of your hangers into this #1 position. Shape the remaining hangers by pulling down on the bottom wire so that they assume a diamond-like shape. These two basic shapes are all that are necessary to build your sculpture.

Choose one bent-wire hanger of the first shape to serve as the sturdy base of your sculpture. Add a second hanger, of either shape, to this base hanger, intertwining the wires as much as possible. Hold these two hangers in place by using narrow strips of adhesive tape to join the points where the wires of each hanger touch one another.

Your sculpture is built hanger-by-hanger. Always secure each additional hanger to an earlier one by means of strips of adhesive tape. Whenever you add a new hanger, tilt it so that the curved hook falls within the sculpture, near its center. Build your piece upward and outward until it takes on a balanced and likable shape. At this early stage, your sculpture will look like a wire skeleton!

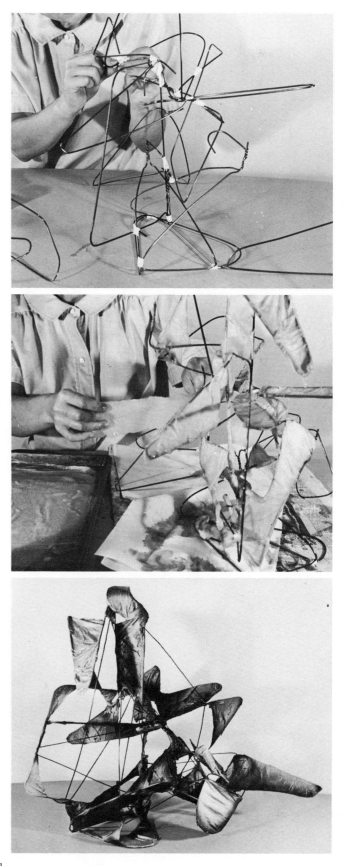

Next, tear sheets of paper towels into strips about 6″ wide. Soak them in liquid starch, keeping them as flat as possible. (A cookie tin is ideal for immersing them.) Lift out a single strip and run your fingers down it to remove the excess starch. Stretch this strip between two sections of wire and wrap the leftover ends around the wire to secure them. Continue to stretch strips between many wires, but do not cover them completely. To keep an open look to your sculpture you can add some pieces of string, dipped in starch, and wind them throughout the piece.

Your finished sculpture should have a light and airy look, rather than a heavy, closed look. Place your completed sculpture on a thick pad of newspaper to catch all the starch that will drip as it dries.

Your Hanger-Up Sculpture can be painted with ordinary poster or house paints, but spray paints are easier to use for their fine spray of color covers all those inner, hard-to-reach spots. If you like the look of welded metal, spray your piece with a combination of black paint and highlight it with gold or copper paint.

41

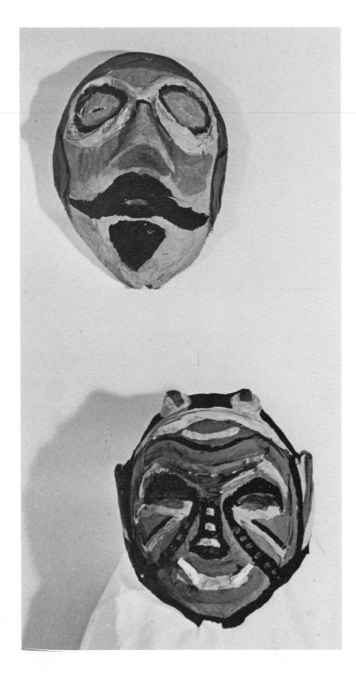

MASKS FROM BALLOONS

shape two masks at one time

IT'S ALWAYS a good idea to know how to construct a mask, for this knowledge often comes in handy. There are times when you might need a mask for Halloween or to portray a character in your school play. Perhaps you'd like to make a mask just to decorate a wall in your room.

This project describes how to make two masks at one time. You can use both masks for yourself, or you can share one with a friend. For materials you'll need a large oval-shaped balloon, newspaper, paper towels, liquid starch, a bowl, rubber bands, scissors and paints.

First, blow up your balloon to face size. Fasten the end closed with a rubber band. Then cut or tear newspaper into strips about 1″–2″ wide. Allow these strips to soften in liquid starch for at least ten minutes. Pick out a single strip of newspaper and paste it to your balloon. Add more of these strips, one by one, pasting them in the same direction as the first strip, until the balloon is covered.

Paste on three more layers of newspaper, strip by strip. Each time you add a new layer, change the direction of the strips. This gives your mask maximum strength. After you build up four newspaper layers, add two more made from strips of paper towels. These final two layers will give you a smooth finish for the painting step which comes later.

Allow this six-layered balloon to dry for at least two or three days. When it feels dry, release the rubber band and the shriveled balloon will drop out. Then pencil a line around the starched shell form to divide it into equal halves. Cut along this guide line with scissors. You'll now have two identical oval shapes, each of which can become a mask. It's up to you to fashion a "personality" for your mask. Will you create an imaginary creature or will you make a famous person? Will your mask be fierce or will it be angelic? When you've decided on your "personality," you can shape the features with narrow strips of starch-soaked paper towels. Build up eyes, noses, horns, teeth, lips, ears, hair or hats . . . it's up to you! Allow the masks to dry once more, and then paint them with poster paints or house enamels.

The final steps are to cut slits for seeing through the eyes and puncturing tiny holes, at the earline, to attach strings for holding the mask on.

Tired of being the same old self? Then put on a mask and be someone else!

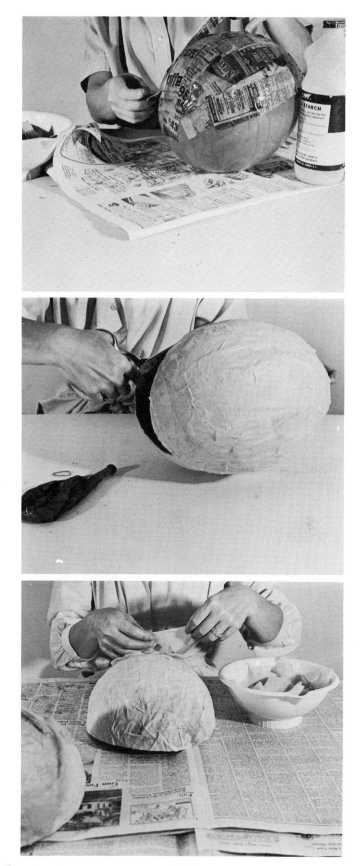

MULTIPLES

abstract designs traced from outline

INTERESTING ABSTRACT PICTURES can be created by tracing different outline forms and interweaving and overlapping them into different arrangements. And what is a better source for such outlining forms than your attic?

First of all, collect several small objects that can be easily traced around, such as a knife, fork, spoon and a bell, or puzzle pieces, nutcrackers and scissors. You'll also need drawing paper and some crayons or colored felt-tipped pens.

Select an object and place it anywhere on your drawing paper. Trace around it making an outline. Move the object to a new spot; place it at a different angle than before and trace around it once more. Choose other objects, tracing around them and overlapping their outlines with those drawn earlier. Change their position on your paper as much as possible. Continue to outline different objects until your paper is full of tracings from edge to edge.

The next step is to create patterns within these traced outlines. For this step, you can use paints, crayons, colored pencils or felt-tipped pens. I like to draw with felt pens for their narrow pen point allows me to include many small details. Now draw patterns within each section of your outline. Draw stripes, checks, solids, polka dots or design some never-been-seen-before patterns of your very own. Be sure not to repeat the same pattern in two neighboring areas. Your design will probably look more organized if you limit your choice of colors to a few instead of using a rainbow-like assortment. Your finished abstract design will be vibrant with pattern and color.

If you think it is fun to make an abstract design using many different object-outlines in one picture, do you think it would be as much fun if you limited yourself to only one or two objects? It's just as much fun. Try it!

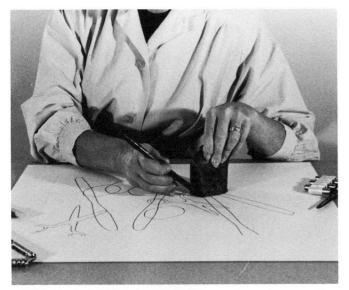

SGRAFFITO

a drawing, painting and etching technique

SGRAFFITO IS THE NAME given to an etching technique that uses a pointed tool to scratch through a covered surface to reveal another surface below. This project describes how to apply a thick layer of wax crayons onto a background which is then covered over with a coat of thick, dark paint. Then a pointed tool is used to scratch through that dark surface revealing the bright colors of the coat underneath.

For materials you'll need wax crayons, dark poster paint (or India ink), a pointed tool for etching and a stiff material such as a floor tile or piece of cardboard for the background.

Begin by coloring your background with irregularly-shaped areas of bright colors, using wax crayons. As you color, bear down hard on your crayons so as to leave behind a thick layer of wax. Fill in your background completely until no uncolored speck can be seen.

The next step is to coat the entire crayoned surface with poster paint or India ink, in your darkest color. You can also use dark wax crayons but I've found that the best results are obtained from paint or ink. As you apply the dark paint, the color should disappear completely. If you can still see color through the dark paint, your surface needs a second coat. Wait for the paint or ink to dry and then go on to the next step.

Select a pointed tool for etching your Sgraffito. This tool can be a knitting needle, a toothpick, a hatpin or a long nail. You'll soon discover that almost any slightly-pointed instrument will scratch through the paint layer to reveal the layer of color underneath. Experiment with different tools to see what kinds of lines they create. Draw your picture directly on the paint with one of these tools, using fine and broad strokes.

As you work along be sure to etch just deep enough to penetrate the dark layer. Be careful that you do not dig deeper into the background material itself.

When you try Sgraffito the next time, why not limit your crayons colors to two or three instead of working with many colors? Try it. You'll like the results!

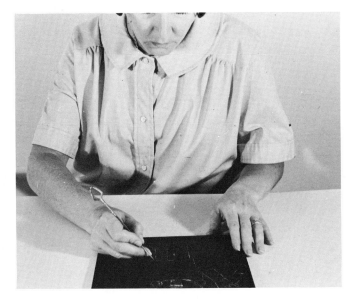

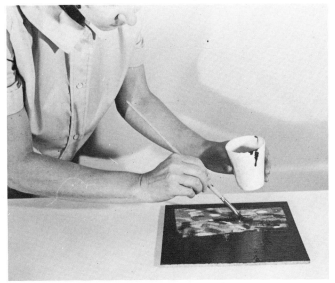

STAMP PAD STAMPINGS

a simple method of relief printing

STAMP PAD STAMPINGS is a kind of relief printing that is fun and simple to do. Once you've tried it, you'll learn that it is good for picture-making and for designing other things such as greeting cards and wrapping paper.

The materials you'll need are one or two inked stamp pads (black plus one other color is good) and hard objects for printing such as a key, can opener, plastic bottles, bits of hardware, hair curlers and even your own fingertips! You'll also need paper to print on, some newspaper and some paper towels for cleanup.

Place your printing paper on some flat surface, such as a table, and then slip a thick pad of newspaper under it. This newspaper will help make your printing surface "bouncier" and thus better for printing than a hard, unbending surface.

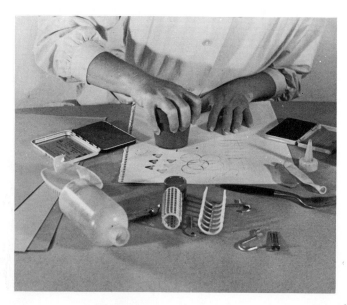

Select one of your printing objects. Press this object into the ink-moistened stamp pad, rolling it slightly from side to side to ink it completely. Press this inked object to your paper, again rolling it from side to side in order to make a complete impression of its inked surface. Make a second print before you reink the object.

Experiment with all your objects and try different ways to create patterns. What sort of a pattern do you get from printing one object-print over another object-print? What happens when you print one color over another? Explore all the ways of combining prints and colors to create original, exciting patterns.

When you are finished printing, be sure to wipe the ink from all the objects that you've used with paper towels.

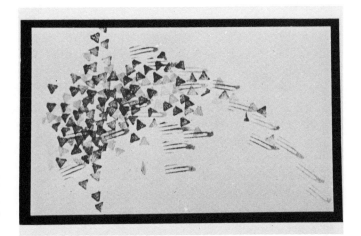

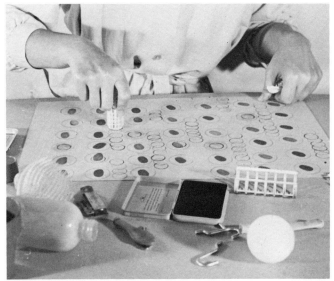

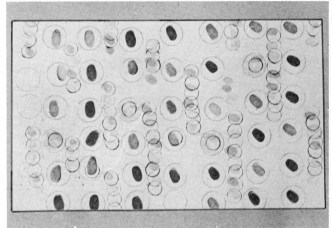

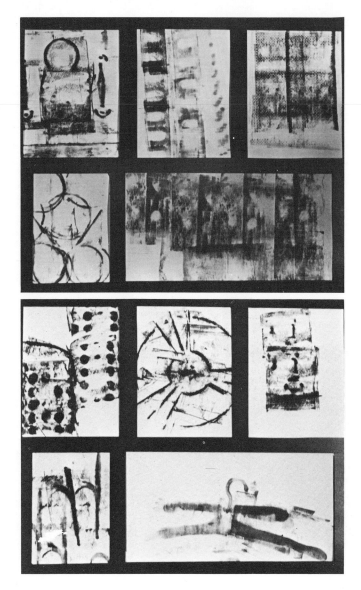

ATTIC PRINTS

relief printing from found surfaces

THIS EXCITING PRINTING PROJECT shows you how an inked brayer (a roller for printing) and some paper can record all kinds of unusual textures that can be found in your attic or in any other storage area. In this method of printing, you'll roll an inked brayer over a textured surface that has been covered with a sheet of paper. The ink transfers an impression of that covered-up surface to paper, making it visible. Once you've tried this simple method, you'll want to search all over your house for textures interesting enough to record on paper.

For materials you'll need a brayer, printing ink and paper.

To start, find some very rough surface such as a straw basket or an old, wooden ceiling beam. Place a piece of paper over this surface and hold it in place with one hand as you roll your inked brayer back and forth over it.

You'll see an impression of that covered-up surface appear immediately! Then try a print of the hinges on an old steamer trunk. Compare that print with a lock print from a more modern suitcase. Make a print of the brass andirons tucked away in some far corner or try a print taken from some wooden hangers. "Print" the wire basket on an electric fan or experiment with a print taken from the carved edge of a piece of furniture.

You'll want to assure your mother that, although you are working with printer's ink, you are not soiling anything. Remind her that a sheet of paper always lies between your inky brayer and the object that you are printing from.

There's no limit to the number and variety of prints that you can make in this way. Try making a print of everything in sight.

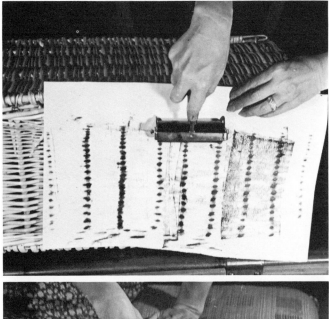

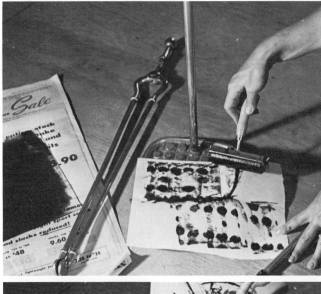

TEAR AND TELL

pictures torn from newspaper

DID YOU EVER want to make a picture only to discover that you were out of paint and crayons? And, to make things worse, you couldn't even locate some scissors and construction paper. Don't dismay! You can still make a wonderful picture if you can find some newspaper, paste, and a piece of dark paper for the background.

First, turn to the classified section of the newspaper. This section is used in Tear and Tell pictures, for its long columns and photoless pages make it ideal for this project. Think about, and decide upon, a subject for your picture. Then, with some part of your picture in mind, tear a shape from the newspaper. Use your nimble fingers to tear the paper so that it becomes a person, a table, a boat or whatever your particular picture needs. Imagine! You've made your fingers become a pair of scissors! Tear, tear, tear many pieces, until your picture is completed.

Then arrange these torn, shaped pieces on your dark background. Move them around until you think they are in the right position to tell your story. Then you can paste these pieces to the background. Use just enough paste to stick them; too much paste will only ooze out at the edges.

Not all your pieces need be pasted flat. You can build up texture in your picture in several ways. For example, you can paste pieces of newspaper on top of other pieces to create a thickness or you can curl, pleat or fold pieces of newspaper. Keep your background plain and simple, for the newspaper will show up more effectively against an uncluttered background.

And there it is—a picture made from practically "nothing"!

HODGEPODGE COLLAGE

a composition made from odds and ends

AN ARRANGEMENT of things that are pasted together is called a collage. When that arrangement is whimsically put together from odds and ends, I call it a Hodgepodge Collage. Using odds and ends for picture-making will open your eyes to the beauty and usefulness of things which so often end up in the wastebasket. It's also fun to take an everyday item and give it a witty new "life." For example, the zipper on your jacket has the job of holding the two sides closed. In a Hodgepodge Collage, however, a zipper could become the trunk of a tall tree, or the steel of train tracks or even the spindly legs of a skeleton. Everything that you find and collect can take on another useful personality in a collage.

Before you can start your picture-making, you must first stock up with a collection of "things." (There's no limit to the kinds and amounts of things that you can gather, once you get started!) Try to include some of the following: bits of yarn, odd-shaped buttons, broken zippers, scraps of fabric, knitting needles, plastic bobbins, greeting cards, theater programs, paper doilies, game parts, gummed stickers, ribbons, Christmas trim, ends of wallpaper, string or pieces of leather. You'll also need a piece of paper or cardboard for the background and glue. Once you have some (or all) of these "things," you can begin to experiment with subject ideas.

Select some objects at random and arrange them on your background. Move them around or exchange them for other things until an idea for a picture is suggested to you. Rearrange and change things until your arrangement of objects satisfies you. Always try for the greatest variety of thicknesses, color and texture in every picture that you make. Contrast smooth paper with rough leather, or use flat, delicate lace next to thick, wooden puzzle parts. Glue this arrangement of objects to your background.

Sometimes the idea of a story-telling collage can be made clearer by adding cutout figures of people or animals, taken from pages of old, discarded magazines. When these figures are in your collage, they often supply the necessary ingredient to help viewers understand what you are saying in your picture.

DIORAMAS

assembled from premolded shipping forms

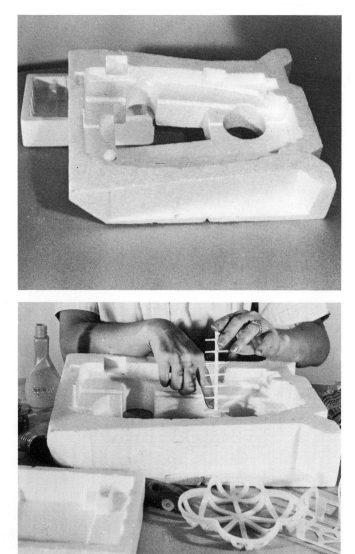

WHEN TELEVISION SETS, radios and cameras are packed for shipment, they often are held securely within their carton by a thick, foamy plastic material which has been molded around them. This shipping form is the stimulating basis for a Diorama.

First, you must locate one of these packing pieces. If you can't find one around your house, ask a friendly shopkeeper to save one for you. When you've found your shipping piece, study its shape well.

Stretch your imagination to turn this shipping piece into something new and unique. Could this plain white form become a lunar city? Or could it be shaped into a children's zoo? If you added racing cars and guardrails could it become a speedway? Once you've decided upon the theme for your Diorama, scout around for the right odds and ends that will turn it into the Diorama of your imagination.

All kinds of ordinary, everyday materials can become something different in a Diorama. For example, plastic containers for vegetables become fences and walls, and checkers or marbles pave streets. Sometimes small boxes become houses and stables and burnt-out flashbulbs become bushes. Every scrap you use is turned into something new, in miniaturized form.

When you are constructing your Diorama, you can usually keep things in place by pressing part of them into the soft plastic material. Figures of people, animals and vehicles can be clipped from magazines and mounted on cardboard to add to your Diorama. You will want to glue some things in place permanently, but it will be much more fun if you leave things like cars and people unglued so that you can move them around your Diorama while you tell a story.

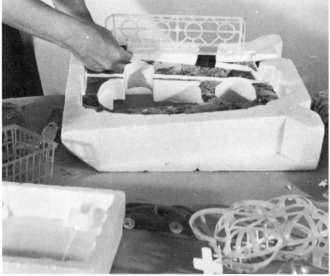

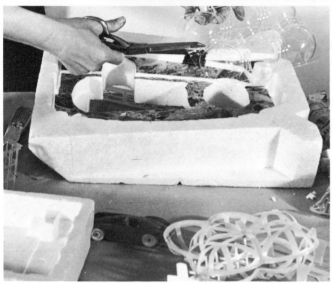

MOBILES IN ORBIT

moving sculpture assembled from magazine illustrations

THIS MOBILE IN ORBIT "floats" in the air, and even in the faintest breeze, its shapes-within-shapes turn and twist actively. It starts from a single sheet of cardboard which has been covered on both sides with illustrations clipped from magazines. The cardboard is cut apart and reassembled to produce ever-changing forms and pictures.

For materials you'll need a sheet of cardboard for each mobile (the illustrations show two mobiles; one is rectangular, the other circular), colored paper or full-page illustrations from magazines, scissors, ruler or compass, paste and a needle with thread.

Begin by covering both sides of the cardboard in one of the following ways:
—paste full-page magazine illustrations on both sides, or
—paste plain paper on one side, patterned paper on the reverse side or
—paste light paper on one side, dark paper on the reverse side.
Then choose one of these basic shapes for your mobile —a rectangle, a square, a circle or a diamond. Draw this shape (with compass or ruler as needed) as large as will fit onto your covered cardboard. This will be the outline of your finished mobile.

Mark the center point of this outline. Now draw a smaller outline on the cardboard, 1½″ closer to the center. Repeat this reducing-and-drawing, making each outline about 1½″ smaller than the one before. The smallest shape probably should not be less than 2″–3″ across. You will need a total of three, four or five shapes-within-shapes.

Now cut out the outlines you have drawn. Then trim ¼″ from the outside edge of all the pieces. This trimming step is very important in later achieving a mobile

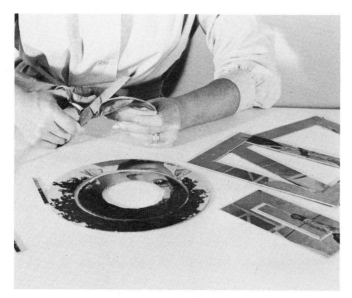

with free-moving parts. Reassemble all the pieces on a flat surface so that your outline looks as it did before being cut apart. Draw a faint line from the exact center straight up to the top of your outline. The stringing is done along this line.

In order to string your mobile together, you begin with the smallest, innermost piece and work out toward the largest piece. Thread a needle with a long thread, knotted at one end. Pass the needle through the top of the smallest piece, as close to the edge as possible, on your faint "stringing line." Pick up the second piece and pass the needle through it, as close to its lower edge as possible, on the "stringing line." Make a knot between the two pieces so that the first piece dangles freely. Pass the needle through the second piece, as close to its upper edge as possible, on the "stringing line." (Do not make a knot at this point; knots are used only to keep an upper piece from sliding down onto a lower piece.) Pick up the third piece and pass the needle through it as you did on the second piece. Continue to add the remaining pieces by string and knotting as before. After you've knotted the last piece in place, be sure to leave a length of thread for hanging.

Now hang up your mobile and study its turning motion. Does it move freely? If so, you need not make any adjustments. Do some pieces bump one another? If so, see if they have been trimmed enough or if they have been strung properly. Adjust the string or the trimming so that your mobile will move easily in the slightest breeze.

To begin, cut many pieces of wire into different lengths from 5″ to 16″ long. You'll need at least 15 pieces of wire. Bend each wire in the following shape: starting at the center, use pliers to bend a small loop which points upward. Then, at each end of the wire, bend loops that face downward. Don't bend the end loops to a closed position, for this is done as a later step. Bend all your wire pieces into this shape before you continue to the next step. A mobile of this type begins with its lowest wire to which are added other wires, working upward toward its highest wire at the hanging point. (Generally, the lowest wire is also the shortest wire.)

Remove any strings or clips which may be attached to the identification tags. Select one of the short wires; hang a tag on each end by threading it onto a partially open loop. Now close the loop with your pliers. Choose a second wire of a different length. This time connect one of its end loops to the center loop of the first wire. Close the loop that joins these two wires. Then add a tag to the empty end for balance and close that loop. Your mobile grows by this linking and balancing of wires and balance pieces.

There is a good deal of similarity between balancing a mobile and trying to balance on a seesaw with a friend who weighs more than you do. You can balance one another, even though your weights are not equal, if you shift your weight back and forth toward the center of the seesaw. Sometimes your mobile is quite balanced and then, as you increase its size, you add a wire with tags that makes it tilt. So you must balance it once more, by adding more weight to the other side.

In its early stages, while it is still small, you'll be able to hold your mobile in one hand as you work upon it with the other. But, as it grows larger and more complicated, it must be suspended so that you can work upon it and, at the same time, judge its balance and beauty.

The very best way to understand how to build and balance a bent-wire mobile is to make one yourself. Do try it. It's lots of fun!

TAG MOBILES

animated sculpture made from bent wire

THIS PROJECT describes how a mobile can be constructed from bent-wire pieces. Colored, round identification tags hang on the ends of the wires to balance the sculpture. Once you understand the principles of construction, assembly and balance, you can go on to create other such sculptures, substituting various materials in the place of the identification tags called for in this project.

The materials you'll need are medium-weight wire, pliers and colored identification tags.

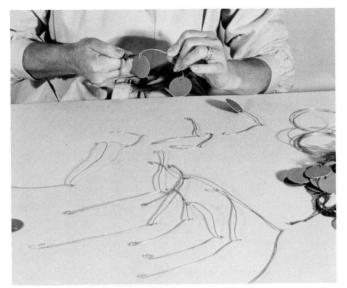

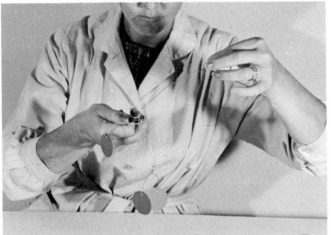

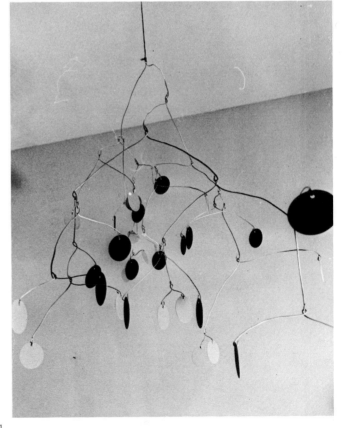

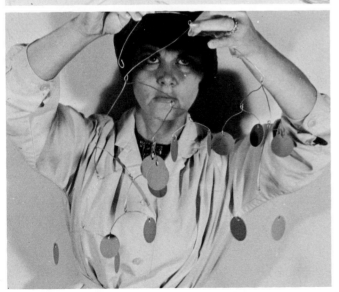

61

CIGAR HOLDER SCULPTURES

an experiment with fused plastics

IN ORDER TO CONSTRUCT a piece of sculpture like the one in the picture, you will have to know some cigar smokers. Then you'll have to find one among them who prefers cigars of the plastic-tipped variety. Ask your cigar smoker to save the next 30 or 40 plastic holders for you.

When you have amassed such a hoard, soak them overnight in soapy water in order to remove any remnants of tobacco left inside the tips. Drain, rinse and dry the holders. The rest of the materials can be gathered when the tips are drying.

For the base you'll need a block of wood or cork. You'll also need a short piece of stiff wire, kitchen tongs and a candle. When I experimented with different brands of cigar tips, I found that they are all non-flammable as they certainly ought to be! Even so, an

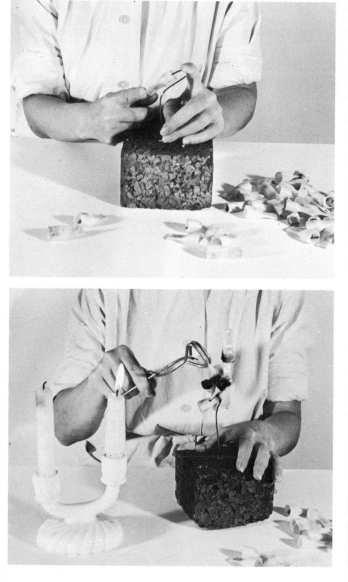

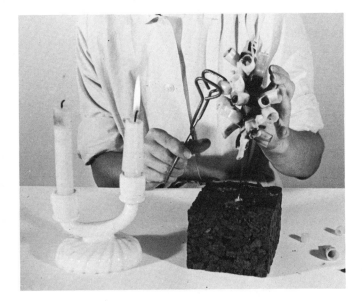

adult should always be present when you are working with a lighted candle. As an extra security measure, also use the tongs while melting and fusing the tips, to guard against possible mishaps and scorched fingers.

For assembling your structure, you can substitute strong glue instead of melting the tips in the candle flame if you prefer. However, if you glue your sculpture together, instead of fusing it, the pieces will remain uniformly cream-colored rather than develop the carbon black areas produced by the flame.

Begin the sculpture by inserting a short, stiff piece of wire into the wood or cork base. Bend the wire slightly at the tip. Thread the wire through the hole in the plastic tip; the bend in the wire holds the tip suspended from the base. It is upon this first tip that the rest of the sculpture will be built. Using tongs, pick up a second plastic tip. Hold either end of it in the candle flame. Keep it there until it appears to soften and begins to blacken. Press this warm, softened piece to the first tip, mounted on the wire. Hold the pieces together, for a moment, until they stick and fuse to one another.

Your sculpture grows in size by building it up piece by piece, that is tip by tip, steadily adding to its height and width. You can vary its shape by fusing the plastic tips at different angles, or you can even nestle small tips within larger ones.

Turn your sculpture as you work so that it will have balance and form when viewed from all sides. The final size and shape of your sculpture will be determined only by your own imagination and the number of tips with which you have to work.

PLASTIC BOX STENCILING

a dry brush technique

MANY ARTISTS like to work with their brushes fairly dripping with paint. But there is another perfectly good painting technique that starts with a brush that has very little paint on its bristles. This technique is called "dry brush" painting, and our project combines this with a stenciling technique to create unusual designs on paper from ordinary plastic fruit and vegetable containers with holes.

For this project you will need a few plastic fruit or vegetable containers, house paint or poster paint in one or two colors, a stiff straight-edged brush, newspaper and white or colored paper.

Before you begin to stencil, you must prepare your brush so that it has the proper amount of "dryness." First, dip the tip of your brush into paint lightly. Then work the brush back and forth on a thick pad of newspaper until most of the paint comes off. When you can see individual marks made by the hairs of the brush, you'll know that you've removed enough paint. Even though your brush is termed "dry," you'll be amazed to see how many designs you can stencil with the tiny amount of paint remaining within the bristles.

Choose one of the plastic boxes. Look at it and you'll discover that a single box contains several different designs. Usually the pattern on the ends of the box differs from the patterns on its sides and bottom. Place your box on white or colored paper and hold it in place with one hand. Then stab your almost-dry brush at the grillwork design of the plastic box with a vigorous, repeated, up-and-down motion. This stabbing action allows the paint to penetrate the paper while the grillwork of the plastic blocks out certain areas of that paper, creating a stenciled design. Lift the plastic container carefully and study this stenciled design.

Once you have mastered this simple technique, you can go on to explore further with design and color. Try stenciling one color over another or one design on top of another. Does your stencil change if you use a rough paper instead of a smoother paper? The excitement really begins when you begin to experiment with design, color and texture.

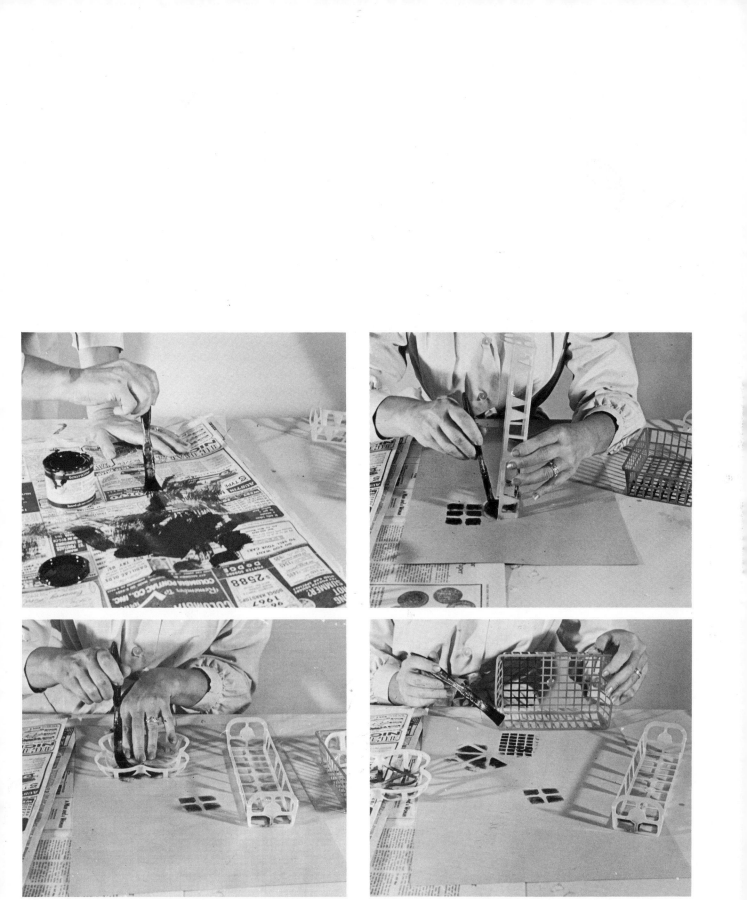

CORRUGATED PICTURES

painted optical illusions

THERE ARE some kinds of paintings that try to fool your eye, leading you to believe that a picture is moving, while it is not moving at all! There are many ways to achieve this optical illusion, most of which are quite complicated. This project shows you a simplified way to create an optical motion effect. And it goes one step further, in that this Corrugated Picture (which already makes your eye jump a little) has parts which actually do turn and move within the picture!

The materials needed are a large sheet of corrugated cardboard and a similar-sized sheet of smooth cardboard, some round objects, like cans or plates, a pencil, two colors of paint, scissors, paste and two or three paper fasteners.

First trace around your round objects, outlining several circles on the sheet of corrugated cardboard. While you are tracing the circles, overlap some of them. Then trace some square-edged shapes onto the same cardboard, overlapping them with some of the circles.

The next step is to prepare your paints, making a third, blended color from the original two colors. Take a small portion of each of the starting colors and mix them together. This mixing gives you three related colors.

Your ridged cardboard background has already been divided into geometrical shapes by tracing and overlapping circles and squares. Consider each divided part of every circle or square as a separate area. Each area will be painted in its own individual way, using only three colors in various combinations of solids and stripes. Let us assume that your three "colors" are black, white and gray. With these colors, and using the ridges of the corrugated as guidelines for stripe-making, you can pattern in the following ways: you can paint some areas all black, all white or all gray or you can paint black and white stripes, gray and white stripes or gray and black stripes.

To create the best optical effects, all touching areas must be a different solid or striped pattern. Painting a Corrugated Picture takes thought and time, but it is well worth the effort when you see bold designs emerge from this careful planning.

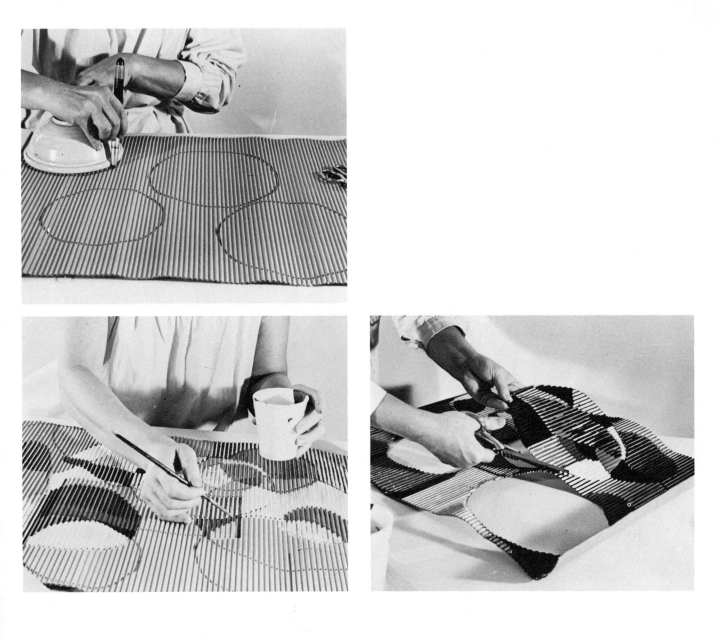

Allow the painted cardboard to dry thoroughly. Then cut out two or three whole circles from it. Paste the remaining sheet (from which the circles have been cut) to the smooth sheet of cardboard. Now, push paper fasteners through the centers of the cutout circles and fasten these circles back into place on the larger, painted cardboard. Touch up the brass heads of the paper fasteners with a dab of matching paint so that they blend in with their surroundings.

Your finished Corrugated Picture will be very "active"! You can make it "jump" a little more by turning some of the circles so that their stripes are at angles to other striped areas.

PRINTS FROM PLASTER

a printing technique

THIS PRINTING PROJECT starts with a thin slab of plaster which has been cast from a milk carton mold. Using plaster for your printing block is an excellent idea for it is inexpensive, it can be easily engraved and it lasts a long time.

For materials you will need plaster of paris, a cardboard milk carton in quart or half-gallon size, printing ink, a brayer (an ink roller), a pointed tool for etching, a sheet of cardboard for rolling out the ink, scrap paper and a pencil and colored or white paper for printing.

First, you must cast your printing block from plaster. Mix enough plaster to fill a milk carton to a thickness of 1½" – 2". Pour the plaster into the carton and allow it to harden overnight. When the plaster feels dry, tear off the cardboard carton. (The plaster will not stick to the plastic-coated inner lining of the carton.)

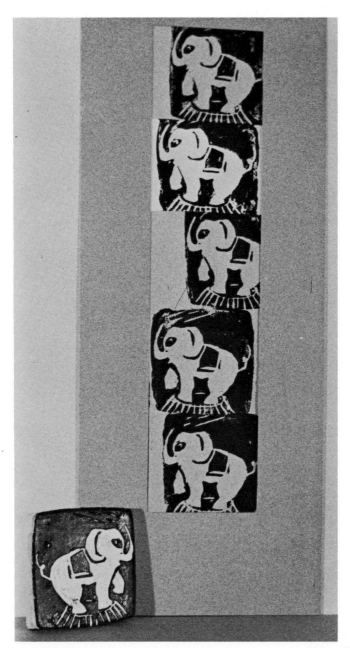

Plan a simple design or picture on scrap paper. Transfer this design to your plaster block by drawing it directly or by using carbon paper. Then use a pointed tool (a long nail or screwdriver) to engrave your picture or design into the soft plaster along these drawn lines. Coat your brayer with ink and roll this brayer over the engraved plaster block. Vary your direction of rolling ink so that the block is totally covered with an even application.

Place a sheet of paper on top of the ink and rub your palm over the paper in a circular motion. This kind of rubbing motion is called burnishing and transfers the ink from your printing block to your paper to create a print. Peel off the paper slowly and examine your first print. You may have "pulled" a perfect print on your first try but, more likely, your first prints will not be your best prints. It takes a little experimenting before you know how much to ink a block and how much to burnish a print.

To make more prints simply reink your block. Keep "pulling" prints until you get several good ones. A single block of plaster lasts a very long time before it starts to wear out. If you want to, you can make two hundred or more prints from one block before it begins to crumble. You can see why it is an excellent way to make posters and greeting cards!

WEATHER STRIPPING PRINTS

impressions from felt strips

HERE'S AN INEXPENSIVE and readily-found material that needs little preparation to be made into an excellent printing substance. When this thick felt material is glued to a background and inked thoroughly, its highly-raised surface makes an ideal relief-type printing plate.

For this project you'll need a few feet of weather stripping, glue, scissors, stiff cardboard, household paints (or printing ink), a brayer (an ink roller) and paper for printing.

First, decide whether you will make an abstract design print or a print with a realistic theme. An abstract design is created easily by snipping a length of weather stripping into small, geometrical shapes such as rectangles, triangles, diamonds or squares. These shapes are arranged and glued onto a sheet of stiff cardboard, forming a pleasing abstract design.

A realistic picture starts from an outline of your subject drawn on stiff cardboard. (Keep it simple and work as large as possible.) The weather stripping is then cut into strips to fit the contours of your outline. Next, these pieces are glued securely to the cardboard to create the printing plate.

Spoon out some household paint (or squeeze out some printing ink) onto a thick piece of cardboard. Roll the brayer back and forth in the paint until it is well "inked." Then roll this brayer over the felt weather

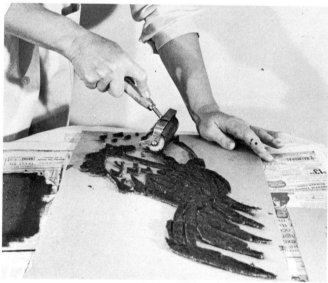

stripping printing plate. When you do this, only the felt receives the ink because it is raised higher than the cardboard on which it is mounted. This method of printing is known as relief printing.

Place a sheet of paper over the inked surface. Rub the paper hard with the palm of your hand, making a circular motion. Peel off the paper slowly and examine your first print. Usually the first few prints will be uneven until the weather stripping becomes thoroughly "seasoned" (inked). Reink your plate and try other prints until you "pull" a perfect one.

This method of printing is good for making a single print or dozens of prints. Even the used, once-inked weather stripping plates are attractive enough to frame as pictures once you are finished printing with them.

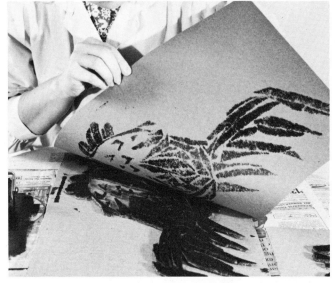

FUNNY FACE PICTURES

a collage made from nuts and bolts

WITH A HANDFUL OF HARDWARE, a bit of paint and a lot of imagination, you can make a Funny Face Picture like this. You'll find that the method is easy and the materials required are few.

You'll need a piece of plywood (or very heavy cardboard), dark household paint, a brush and an assortment of hardware such as nuts, bolts, hinges, curtain hooks, washers, nails, staples and screws.

First, place your plywood on a flat surface. Dip your brush into paint and cover the plywood from edge to edge with a thick, *heavy* coat of paint. Go on to the next step before the paint has a chance to begin to dry.

Choose some pieces of hardware—nails, hooks, screws, nuts or bolts—and arrange your picture by placing these pieces right into the wet paint. Do not move them once they've touched the paint. When the paint dries it will "glue" the hardware firmly to the plywood while, at the same time, provide a dark background which contrasts with the shiny metal of the hardware. No other glue is needed!

Let your imagination take over to create fanciful animals, beautiful flowers or even funny faces. Be sure that your collage is completely dried before you hang it up else the hardware will slide off!

SPARKLING SPACKLE PANELS

3-dimensional reliefs made from found objects

HERE'S A CHANCE to use all those discarded things that you've saved in the garage. This project describes how to manipulate these found objects to create a really different three-dimensional panel in relief. And after you've assembled the panel, you'll be shown how to "antique" its finish so that new plastics and shiny metals suddenly look aged and worn.

You will need a stiff background such as plywood or very heavy cardboard, a box of spackle, newspaper, glue, varnish, metallic paint, a brush and some of the following objects: screws, nails, hooks and other hardware, bottle tops, string, scraps of metal and plastic.

Arrange your collection of found objects on the plywood background in any random pattern. Move the pieces around, arranging and rearranging them until they form a design that pleases you. Your relief will be especially interesting if you emphasize the thickness of objects by placing thick things next to flatter objects and by contrasting sizes by placing large objects next to smaller ones. Glue everything firmly to the plywood with fast-drying glue.

Place your hardware-covered panel on a thick pad of newspaper. Mix up a small amount of spackle, according to the manufacturer's directions. Using a large brush (or even your hand) scoop up some spackle and brush a coat of it over the entire panel. Dab on the spackle so that it covers every object well, but be careful not to drown these objects under a too-heavy coat. The effect you want is a "frosted" panel but not a shapeless relief.

If you were using plaster of paris instead of spackle for this covering step, you'd have to rush your work as fast as possible because plaster "sets up" (hardens) rapidly. Spackle will harden eventually, but it stays softer, and thus more workable, for a longer time.

Allow the spackle-covered panel to dry for several hours or, preferably, overnight. The next step is to create a patina (finish) for your panel. An antique-like effect can be achieved in two simple steps: first, paint or spray paint the entire panel with gold, silver or copper metallic-colored paint. Allow this shiny base coat to dry. Then cover over the metal-painted panel with a coat of varnish in a dark tone. Wipe off the wet varnish immediately, here and there, with cloth or toweling to reveal tiny areas of the sparkling metallic paint below. Remove just enough to highlight parts of your panel.

In a matter of minutes, you've "aged" your work of art by at least 50 years or more!

ACROBAT TOTEM POLES

assembled from discarded bits of lumber

In almost every house, at some time during the year, some carpentry is needed to improve the home's appearance or to make it more comfortable. And after that chore is finished, a lot of odds and ends of lumber are leftover to be discarded . . . or to be claimed for use by you!

If there's no carpentry going on at your house you can get similar blocks of wood by asking at your local woodworking shop. Most carpenters will be glad to give you as much as you want; otherwise, they have to pay to have such remains hauled away. The other materials you'll need are sandpaper, glue, poster paint or house paint.

The object of an Acrobat Totem Pole is not to imitate Indian or Eskimo-style totem poles, but, rather, to build a contemporary sculpture of stacked-up figures. An Acrobat Totem Pole can have as few as two figures; it can also have many more, depending on your wood supply and your ability to construct and balance the figures.

First of all, sandpaper all the rough sides of the wooden blocks. Then, stack some of them together to form a body with head, arms and legs. In constructing this Totem Pole the figures are assembled individually and then stacked together to fashion one larger piece later on.

When you have two or more figures constructed and glued together you can try different arrangements of stacking them up. Try leaning some out at angles to the others. When you like your combination of acrobats, you can glue them together into a single Totem Pole. It will be necessary to support the leaning figures while they are being glued together.

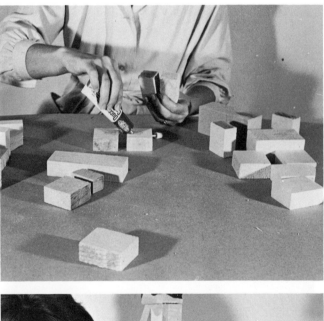

Painting the Acrobats is the next step. Keep your colors thick, especially if you are working with poster paint. Remember, you are decorating "raw," unfinished wood, which will tend to absorb much of your paint. I've found that the best method is to paint all the areas that are the same color (the skin, for example) at the same time. Use your vivid imagination to design colorful, original costumes for your Acrobats. Last, paint in the facial features which give the Acrobats expression.

If you've painted with poster paints, it's a good idea to protect your Acrobat Totem Pole against smudge marks by giving it a final coat of clear lacquer or shellac. Of course balancing Acrobats are only one of many different subjects that can be constructed from blocks of wood. Another time, why not try making animals, towns or even boats?

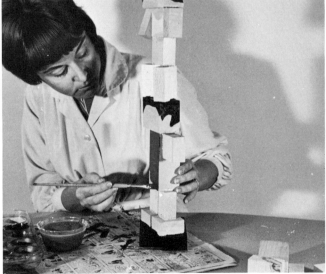

77

HARDWARE JEWELRY

liquid solder binds metal to metal

DID YOU KNOW that many sculptors (who ordinarily sculpt with large clay or stone forms) like to create tiny pieces of jewelry? These artists think of jewelry as small works of sculpture rather than as a mere ornament to hang around your neck or pin onto a dress. This project combines bits of hardware, liquid solder and sometimes parts of old discarded jewelry to whip up original new pieces of jewelry.

To begin, you'll need one or more of the following: the pin back from an old brooch, a chain for hanging a pendant or a pair of earring backs. You'll also need some plastic kitchen wrap, a tube of liquid solder and a variety of small bits of hardware such as carpet tacks, upholstery tacks, nails, screws, nuts, glazier's points, wire, chain or washers. You can even include some pieces of discarded jewelry, bits of colored glass or marbles. Small tweezers would be handy to have (for fussier operations), but they are not necessary.

Making Hardware Jewelry is quite simple. Begin by tearing off a small sheet of plastic wrap and place it flat

on your table. Arrange some pieces of hardware on the wrap, moving them about until their placement pleases you. Squeeze some liquid solder onto the hardware pieces to join them together. Let some of the solder flow onto the plastic wrap. You'll later discover that it will not stick to the plastic and the finished piece of jewelry can be peeled from the plastic once the solder has hardened.

Liquid solder is your most important ingredient in building this type of jewelry. It is the "glue" which holds your jewelry together and, at the same time, adds a dark gray tone which contrasts with the metals used within the pieces. As you build your jewelry, be sure to contrast tones of metal. For example, combine silver nuts with brass screws. Mix shiny tacks with dull washers. When solder is half-hardened, you can scrape it lightly to produce a bark-like texture, or when it has hardened completely, it can be polished to a shiny gloss. This new shape can be turned into a wearable piece of jewelry by adding a pin back, a chain or a pair of earring backs.

Whole pieces of discarded jewelry can also be the start of new pieces of Hardware Jewelry. Any brooch, pendant or earring can act as the base shape upon which a new surface is constructed by adding bits of hardware and "gluing" it all together with liquid solder squeezed from the tube.

Some projects ask you to work quickly and boldly. This one allows you to work slowly and carefully to create a beautiful piece of jewelry that you'd be proud to wear or to give as a present.

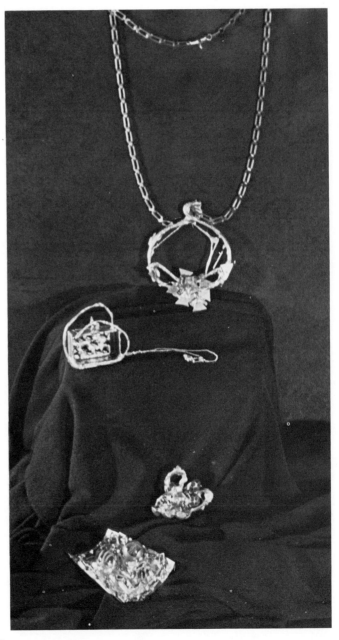

DAIRY CARTON SCULPTURE

carving from a plaster block

THERE ARE TWO basic ways to form a piece of sculpture. One is to start with a small shape of some modeling material and then to build it up by *adding* to it. The opposite way of sculpting is to start with a large shape and then to shape it by taking parts *away* from it. Dairy Carton Sculpture is the second method, for a large block of plaster is gradually chipped away, bit by bit, to shape your particular piece of sculpture.

For materials you'll need a dairy carton in any size, plaster of paris, a screwdriver or flat-edged chisel, a hammer, sandpaper and paints.

First of all, the block of plaster for carving must be cast. This is done by filling an empty dairy carton with plaster of paris. (I would advise beginners to start with a quart-size or half-gallon size carton. The more carving experience you have, the larger the container you can work upon successfully.) It will take from one to four days for the plaster to dry, depending on the size and thickness of your block. When the plaster has dried, you can tear away the cardboard carton.

The next step is to sketch the subject of your sculpture on all sides of the block. Outline your subject as it would look if you were viewing it from the sides or from the back and from the top. When these guidelines are drawn, you are ready to begin carving.

Hold a screwdriver or chisel against the areas where you want to remove plaster. Hit the end of the chisel with your hammer in a tapping-like motion. You'll soon discover that, unlike marble, plaster breaks away easily. It won't be long before you see the very rough shape of your future sculpture emerging from what once was a solid block of plaster.

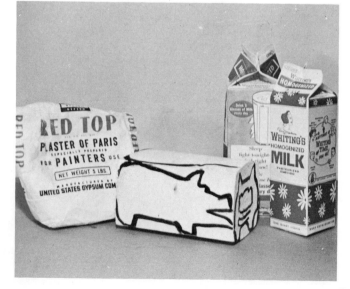

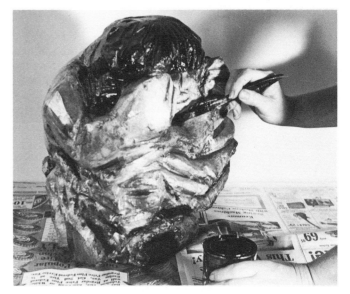

As you chip away at your sculpture, turn it frequently so that you can shape it a little at a time on all four sides. Keep chipping away until your sculpture is at an almost-finished shape. Working with plaster is always a messy business, no matter how neat you try to be. Try to wear old clothes and carve outside if possible. If you must work inside, cover your floor well with newspaper to protect it.

The final smoothing and shaping can be done with sandpaper, unless you prefer to keep the rough marks made by your chisel or screwdriver. Your finished piece can be left in its natural-white plaster color or it can be painted. When I looked at my finished sculpture, the "Stubborn Child," I decided that it would look best if I toned it with paints and varnishes.

CASTING FROM PUTTY

impressed designs are cast with plaster

THIS PROJECT shows you how to produce a design in a soft putty mold and then to reproduce this design by casting plaster in the mold. You'll find that putty is an ideal material to use for it is inexpensive, it takes a designed impression well and its oily surface does not permit plaster to stick to it.

The materials you'll need are a can of putty, plaster of paris, plastic wrap, tinfoil, cardboard, a kitchen knife, wood stain and some objects to make impressions in the putty.

First, spread the putty onto a sheet of plastic wrap which is on top of your cardboard. Roll the putty out flat so that it is approximately 1″ thick. Square off the edges of this flattened piece with a knife.

Then divide this larger piece into six or eight rectangles with a knife. Remove these rectangles from the larger piece, and place them on separate squares of tinfoil or cardboard.

Once the putty has been separated into these individual sections, you are free to travel around to different locales to take putty impressions of unusual surfaces. For example, an impression is made by pressing the putty (mounted on foil) against any interesting surface. Try taking an impression of a manhole cover, the hinge on a door or the straw on summer porch furniture.

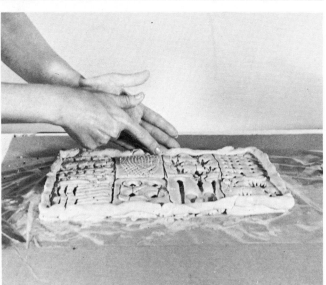

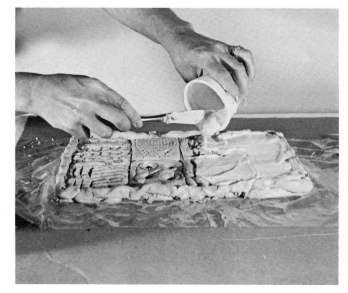

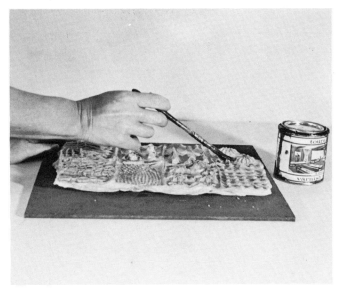

If you are unable to travel around to take such impressions, omit the step which asks you to place the putty on tin foil. Instead, use interesting things found around the garage, like points of tools, edges of hardware or bottle tops, to make designs in the separated rectangles.

Reassemble the separated sections into the original large piece. Push the rectangles together so that their sides touch and all gaps between them are closed. The next step is to build a "retaining wall" of putty around the edge of the large rectangle to help contain the plaster, which you will now use to form designs.

Mix up a batch of plaster and pour it into the putty mold to the height of the retaining wall. Allow the plaster to dry. It can then be removed easily from the putty by simply peeling off the putty mold. You'll see that the plaster has taken a perfect impression from the fine designs that you "printed" into the putty mold.

I like to tone this kind of casting with a thinned-out coat of wood stain as this helps to make the fine designs more visible.

STRIPED ROCKS

a combination of paint and stone

SOMETIMES, in order to fully appreciate the beauty of an object, we must focus our attention on a part of it. This project takes a single stone and uses color and paint to focus on and enhance its natural mineral beauty.

Start with a rock hunt. A short stroll along some city sidewalks or through some leafy woods should make a good beginning for your collection. Search for beautiful stones or pieces of rock that are unusual or varied in color and interesting in shape. It doesn't matter whether your rocks are rough or smooth. Besides the rocks you collect, you will also need paints, a brush and masking tape.

Study one of your rocks. Try to decide how you will divide it into painted and unpainted areas. Which sections have the most striking grain, colors, shine, speckled areas, smoothness or roughness? Are there less interesting areas which, when painted, can serve to frame the more exciting true rock parts?

When you have decided which parts of your stone are to be painted and which are to remain untouched, tear some strips of masking tape and press them onto the rock, making stripes over the area which will be kept unpainted. Each rock will probably be large enough for one to three stripes. You can use horizontal or vertical stripes, or even cross over stripes. The contours of your rock may even suggest that stripes applied at an angle suit it best.

Paint each section left exposed by the tape stripes with a different color. Select your colors to enhance the natural rock colors. For example, use shades of orange or red with pink-tinged rocks or cooler tones of blue and green with dark gray rocks. Allow the paint to dry and then peel off the tape.

If your tape has been applied to a smooth rock it will stick tight and flat against the rock. When the tape is removed, the edges of the stripes will be crisp and straight. If, however, your rock is rough and irregular, the tape edges will be loose in some places and a little paint will seep under the tape. When the tape is removed, the edges of these stripes will be furry rather than straight and smooth.

Either stripe effect is attractive, for it emphasizes the individual character of each rock . . . and that's our purpose: to make the natural beauty of the rock more clear than it was before, by selective painting.

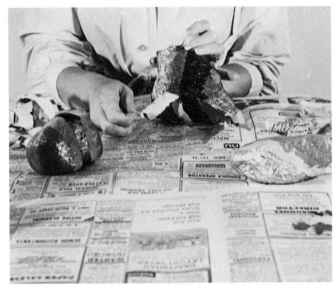

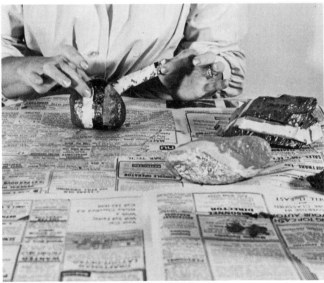

PAINTING WITH DIRT

a painting or a collage?

THE POINT where a painting turns into a collage is often very difficult to determine. Some "paintings" combine paint and paper. Other "paintings" blend paint, paper and cloth. And still others combine paint with natural elements such as dirt, sand and sawdust. These various types of "paintings" are as much a collage as they are a painting.

To begin, you will need house paint in two or three colors, pieces of thick cardboard or plywood for the background and some dirt, sand or sawdust. These natural elements can be combined with each other within a single painting, or they can be used separately in many paintings. How you choose and combine these elements depends on the textural effect you are seeking.

The technique is simple and direct. First, coat your background with a thick layer of house paint. Scoop up one of the natural elements and sprinkle or drop bits of it into the wet paint, guiding your design as you do so. Add a second color of paint if you wish. Dribble or drop paint over parts of the original paint and over some of the textured areas. Paint dribbled on top of dirt, sand or sawdust makes a crust-like surface. Paint dribbled on top of paint will cause the colors to run together. Strangely enough, accidental painting effects (like the running together of colors of paint) are often beautiful and desirable to have in a painting.

Allow your painting to dry in a flat position. You'll discover that any materials scattered earlier in wet paint are now firmly imbedded in it. These natural materials are as much a part of your "painting" as the paints themselves. Is it a collage or a painting?

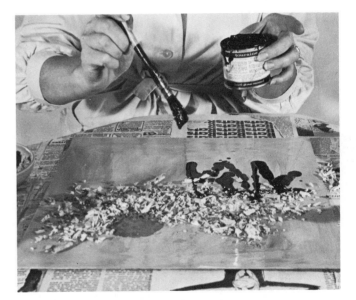

RUB-IT PRINTS

from an ancient technique

STONE RUBBING is an ancient "printing" technique used by Eastern cultures for many centuries to record on paper an impression of some design or textured surface. This project shows you a quick way of adapting this very old method and it simplifies the method.

Rub-It Prints are made by placing a sheet of paper over the surface to be "printed." A dark crayon (or stick of graphite) is rubbed back and forth over the paper. An impression of the textured surface, underneath the paper, appears as you rub the crayon!

You will need sheets of thin paper (typing paper is excellent) and dark wax crayons or a stick of graphite.

Now that you are familiar with the how-to-do method, you can begin to search for surfaces to "print" with this newly-found skill. Did you know that some of the most commonplace things around us have interesting surfaces to be rubbed and recorded?

For example, have you ever taken a "print" of the cracks in the cement sidewalk? Or the bark on an old tree? Does the texture of a brick print differ from that of a wire fence? It does? Prove it! Try taking impressions of a manhole cover or a sidewalk grating. Then try to record the straw on summer furniture or the monogram on engraved silverware.

You can compose a picture out of these various rubbings by combining several prints, in an orderly way, on a single sheet of paper. Or you can even make a game of it. Ask your friends to identify objects from the rubbings. Does this guessing game sound too easy? Try it. It's more difficult than it sounds!

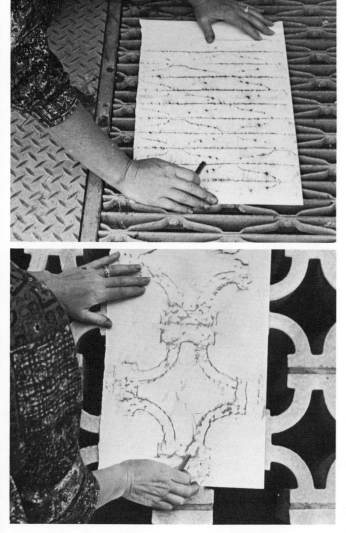

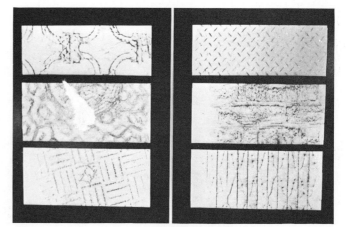

NATURE PRINTS

printing from leaves and weathered wood

No DOUBT you've seen hundred of thousands of leaves in your lifetime. In fact, you've probably picked several dozens of them. But have you ever thought of them as a medium of printmaking?

For materials you'll need different shapes and kinds of leaves, scraps of weathered wood, printing ink, a brayer, a sheet of cardboard for rolling out the ink, old newspaper and paper for printing.

First, cover your table with newspaper. Squeeze out some printing ink onto a sheet of cardboard. Roll the brayer back and forth in the ink until it is evenly coated. Choose one leaf from your collection (perhaps it is wiser not to start with your best leaf until you've had more printing experience), and lay it on the newspaper. Then roll the inked brayer over the whole leaf including its stem. Lift this inked leaf by its stem and transfer it to a clean section of the newspaper. Lay it down, inked side up.

Place a sheet of paper over the leaf. Rub the paper with the palm of your hand using a circular motion. This burnishing transfers the inked impression of the leaf to paper. Peel back the paper carefully and study the results of your first leaf print. Let's hope that you've gotten a perfect print. If you find, however, that your print is too faint, you need to apply more ink. If you see that the delicate vein lines are blurred and lost, you have applied too much.

It takes a bit of experimenting with inking and rubbing before you make perfect prints every time. After a while you'll know instinctively how much is the "right" amount of ink and what is the "right" amount of rubbing that's necessary to produce clear, crisp prints. Now try making some prints from pieces of weathered wood.

After you've made some good prints using one color of ink and one single leaf, you may wish to vary your results by combining inks of different colors and prints of different leaves. You can achieve some dramatic effects by overlapping prints of different colors and prints of different leaves. Try these color-design variations and see what fun Nature Prints can be!

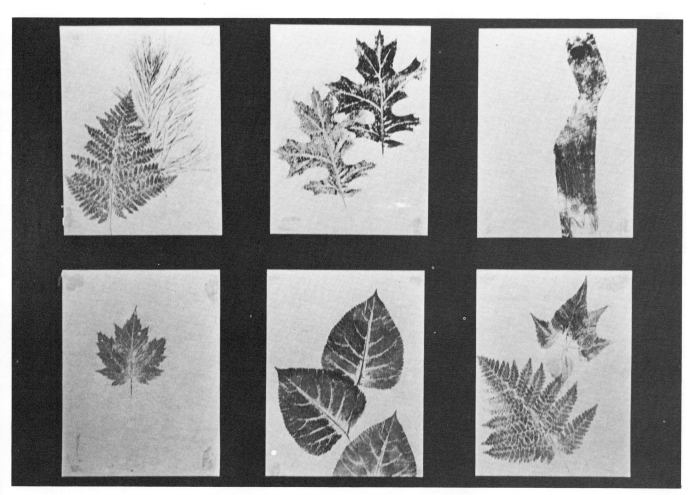

PEBBLE MOSAICS

mosaics from natural materials

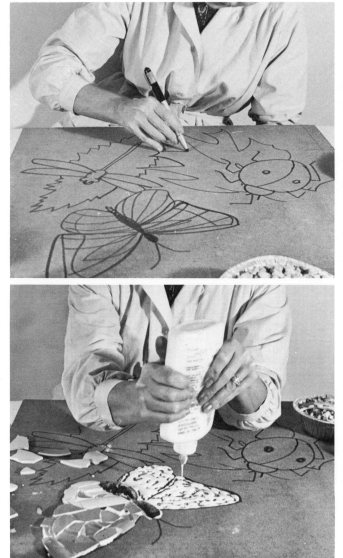

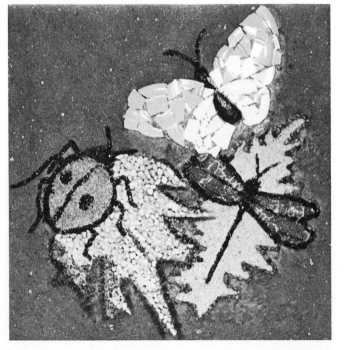

CONSTRUCTING A MOSAIC from natural materials can be as intriguing as putting together a jigsaw puzzle. You'll be amazed how many colorful and inexpensive materials for mosaic-making are waiting to be discovered around your house or backyard. If you hunt around, you'll probably turn up some (if not all) of the following materials: sand, dirt, crushed driveway gravel, sea-shells, pebbles, aquarium and birdcage gravel and even fragments of broken crockery. Continue the search until your collection provides you with a variety of colors and textures. Besides these natural materials, you'll need a piece of plywood for the background and white liquid glue.

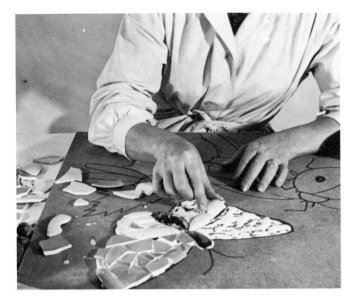

Since your mosaic-making materials are natural things, why not let nature also inspire your subject? Look around the yard or the beach or out the window. Can you see some fluttering leaves or a crawling insect? Can you spot a darting dragonfly or a crawling crab? Make any of these insects, animals or growing things the subject of your mosaic.

Draw your subject directly onto the plywood background with a dark line that can be easily seen and followed. You are now ready to start your mosaic. I've learned that the best method in making a mosaic is to fill in the subject first. I always leave my background to be filled in at the end.

Squeeze out enough glue to cover a small area of your mosaic within those drawn outlines. Fill in that area with pebbles, gravel, shells or bits of crockery, fitting the pieces carefully next to one another. No matter how perfectly you fit these pieces, the white glue will show between them. Therefore, these in-between spots of glue have to be covered up by sprinkling a fine material such as aquarium or birdcage gravel over the wet glue.

Press this fine material into the glue with your hand. Wait a few moments and then remove the excess "filler" by tilting the panel upright *quickly*, allowing the excess material to slide from the panel. You can collect this material for reuse later on.

Continue to squeeze glue, place your materials, fill in and remove excesses until the mosaic is completed, with the exception of the background. Try to contrast colors and textures within your mosaic. An unusual effect comes from using crushed seashells in one of your areas.

Reserve the sand or dirt for filling in the background. When your subject area is completed, you are ready to cover the background by spreading glue over it. Then pour a heavy layer of dirt or sand over the entire panel. Press this material well into the glue. Allow the panel to dry for a day or two before removing the excess dirt or sand.

You may find that you must "scrub" the completely dried panel to rid it of the excess material that still remains. This "scrubbing" will not harm your mosaic (if you do it lightly and if your panel is dry). It will, instead, help to uncover the beauty of your Pebble Mosaic!

FOUND GLASS COMPOSITIONS

new forms for discarded glass

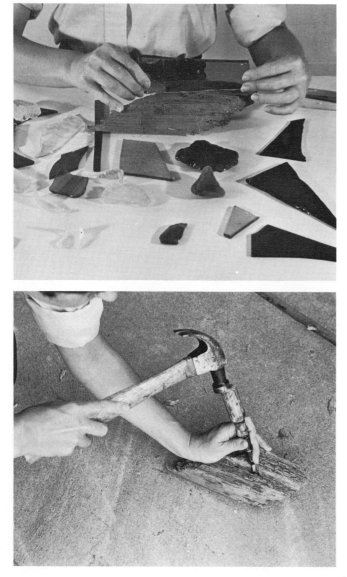

A slow, watchful walk along a beach or even through an alleyway in the city will uncover most of the necessary ingredients for this project. The materials needed are clear and colored fragments of discarded glass, a heavy piece of wood or driftwood, a chisel or cutting device and a strong, clear glue.

Glass found at the beach is "special," for the constant changes of the tide tumble and wash the fragments until they are smooth and their edges rounded. Discarded glass (beach or otherwise) can be found in a variety of colors such as brown, green, blue, frosty white, clear and amber.

First of all, select your longest and flattest piece of glass for the base. This piece is the start of your composition upon which the rest of the glass fragments are glued. This base piece, in turn, rests in a specially dug-out channel in your driftwood base. The piece of driftwood you choose must be even and broad enough on the bottom so as not to wobble or tip over.

Chisel or dig out a 1″ channel in your piece of driftwood as long as your flat base piece of glass. Later on, your glass composition will be placed so that the base piece of glass sits in this channel which has been carved out to its dimensions.

Now you can start to assemble your Found Glass Composition. I've discovered that the best way to work is flat, on a table. This enables you to glue pieces of glass together without much difficulty. Arrange the various pieces of colored glass before you. Study the shape of your driftwood base to see if it suggests a theme for your glass work. Some pieces can be built around a specific idea, others can be, instead, a beautiful arrangement of colored glass pieces.

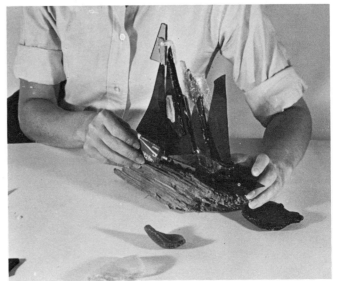

Your composition is constructed by adding and gluing fragments of glass to the base piece of glass, building upward and outward. Keep your entire piece under 12″ in height; glass is very heavy and there is a limit to the weight that ordinary glue will support. Overlap different colors of glass for unusual color effects. The combination of these colors will not be fully appreciated until your piece can be raised from the flat table so light passes through it.

When your composition is completely assembled, allow it to dry overnight. Then fill the channel in the wooden base with glue. Raise your composition upright into this channel. Support the piece until the glue hardens.

Now place your finished Found Glass Composition in front of a window where the light can shine through it.

SPIDER THREADS

a kind of weaving

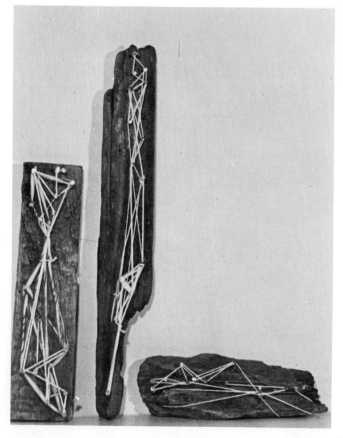

THE SPIDER starts its web with a single, fragile thread and carries it back and forth until he's woven a complicated design. "Spider Threads" imitates the spider's carrying motion, but your woven designs will be much simpler. You'll use yarn and string for your "web-making" materials and, unlike the real spider's web, your kind of weaving can be undone and woven again and again as many times as you want.

For materials you'll need a piece or two of weathered wood, string, yarn or thread and a hammer and some different-sized nails.

Begin by hammering a few nails into each of the three or four corners of your weathered wood piece. Arrange the nails so that they do not stand on soldier-straight lines and place the tallest ones in the center. Vary the number of nails in each corner.

Select a long length of string, yarn or thread. Knot one end of it to any nail and carry the string across to an opposite nail. Wind it around that nail and start back, crossing over to a nail in another corner. Wind it around that nail and go off in another direction. Weave your strands back and forth until they are used up. Always end with a knot tied in a corner, rather than in the center of your "web."

All kinds of weaving variations are possible. For example, you can combine several different types of yarn and string in one "web." You can mix colors of yarns. You can fill your "web" with a lot of weaving or a little weaving. If you don't like the results of your weaving, unwind the strings and start all over!

PEBBLE PARFAIT

rock crushing with a purpose

THIS PROJECT begins with chunks of rocks and whole seashells which are pounded and crushed into a fine gravel. The idea is to collect and arrange this gravel in layers in a clear glass tumbler so as to display the beauty and variety of colors to be found in crushed rocks and shells.

The materials you'll need for this project are rocks, seashells, fragments of building materials such as brick, slate or flagstone, a large rock for pounding, a whisk broom for sweeping up, a slender drinking glass and a wax candle for sealing the top.

To start, select any rock from your collection. Next, find a spot where you can pound this rock without harming any property. A sidewalk, a seawall or a stone stairway are good places to pound rocks. Place the small rock under the larger pounding rock and pound, pound, pound until the little rock crumbles into small pieces. Pound these small bits, again and again, until they are crushed to a fine gravel. Sweep up this gravel and pour a layer of it, about ½″ thick, into the drinking glass.

You'll soon discover that some rocks crumble easily while others refuse to break apart, even with hard pounding. Discard all rocks that do not break apart after you've pounded them once or twice. Seashells crumble very easily and they produce a powder that is nearly as fine as salt.

Choose a second rock, or even a seashell, whose color contrasts with the first rock. Pound this rock until it is reduced to a similar fine gravel. Collect this material and pour a second layer into the glass. As you pour layer upon layer, you will see them form in irregular, up-and-down patterns. Don't try to even them out. The more irregular the patterns of the layers, the more interesting the finished Pebble Parfait will be.

Continue to build up layers until the topmost one is within ¾″ from the rim of the glass. Then light a wax candle (be sure an adult is present when you do) and dribble melted wax over the top layer to seal off the top of your Pebble Parfait. If you've sealed the glass tightly, the multicolored layers will not shift and mix, even if the glass is turned upside down!

FENCE WEAVING

sprucing up a wire fence

FENCE WEAVING can be very colorful or very formal. It can take a few minutes or a few hours. You can weave a fence by yourself, or you can weave one with your friends. You can weave a tiny section or a whole fifty-foot fence. You can weave it and then, if you don't like it, you can take it apart and start all over again!

First of all, the most important material in Fence Weaving is your fence. Look around until you locate a wire fence. But before you start weaving, be *sure* to ask the owner's permission! You can assure him that Fence Weaving will not damage his property in any way. It will, instead, decorate it prettily in a way that no other fence has been decorated before! Then, you must tell the owner that you will remove any decorations that you put up when you are finished. (He may ask you to leave your design!)

Besides your fence you'll need some of the following: crepe paper, tinfoil, newspaper, plastic wrap, ends of fabric, yarn, coat hangers, sticks, tin cans and string.

Choose a spot for each person to weave on that is about two feet or more wide. The weaving is done on the vertical, horizontal or diagonal lines made by the wires of your particular fence. You'll use these wires to wind various things in and out, over and under. Start by selecting one of your materials, such as a strip of colored fabric. Weave this strip through the fence in

any way that looks good to you. Tie on another color of fabric and weave this through the fence so that your weaving spot is longer or wider.

There are no "rules" to Fence Weaving, except to make the fence look as beautiful as you can. You can weave materials so that they are very close to one another or you can leave "holes" in your weaving so that you can see through it. You can dangle things like wire hangers or tin cans by tying them on with yarn or you can fill the wires with loops of newspaper. You can even crumple tinfoil or plastic wrap and stuff it between the wires. If you dangle metal objects they will clank against the wire in a breeze, adding a bit of "music" to your weaving.

After you've worked at your weaving for a while, step back away from it to see how the fence looks from a distance. Chances are, you've turned a dull, plain fence into a huge work of art!

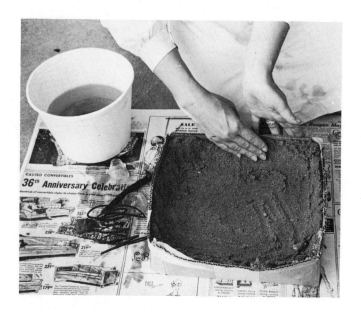

SANDCASTING

casting plaster into sand molds

SANDCASTING is fun to do when you are at the beach. If it's not "beach weather," it's just as much fun to do at home! The directions for making a sandcasting at either the beach or at home are the same, with one exception: when you sandcast at the beach, plaster is poured directly into a depression in the sand. When you work at home, you must first put that sand in a cardboard carton and then, just as before, pour plaster into a hole (the mold) made in the sand.

For materials you'll need a deep, sturdy cardboard carton (for home casting only), a pail for carrying water, plaster of paris, a small piece of wire for a hanging hook, sand and some "tools" for decorating the mold.

At the beach, dig a hole about 6″ deep and about a foot square. At home, half-fill a carton with sand. Wet the sand well with water. Level the bottom of your mold. If you are casting at home, build up the sand around this flat bottom to make "retaining walls" to contain the plaster. (If you are working at the beach, the natural sides of your mold are your "retaining walls.")

Use your fingers, shells, driftwood, a sand shovel, a bottle cap or any object at hand to press shapes into the wet sand. You can also build up bumps and ridges. Remember that your mold is the *reverse* shape of your future casting. What is a "hole" in your sand mold is a "bump" in your plaster casting.

You can even press seashells and beach glass into the mold and leave them there. Later on, when the plaster

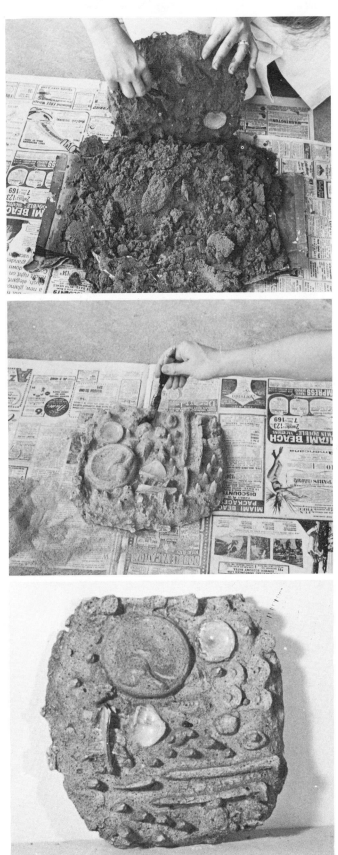

is poured, it will ooze around these solid pieces and they will become a permanent part of your sandcasting.

When your mold is designed, you must mix up a good quantity of plaster of paris. If you are casting at the beach, you can substitute sea water instead of the usual tap water that is needed. Pour the liquid plaster into your sand mold slowly and carefully so that the design is not disturbed. Fill your mold to a thickness of 2″–3″.

Twist a wire loop and insert it into the wet plaster for a hanging hook. Now the casting must dry. This will take a few hours in very bright sunshine or two or three days if you are working indoors.

When your sandcasting feels dry, it can be removed from its mold. Tear away the cardboard carton or dig it up from the beach. When you have freed it from its mold, you'll see that a good deal of sand still remains on its face. Carefully brush away this excess sand until you uncover the plaster. Of course, some sand always remains imbedded on the face of your casting, giving it an ancient, weathered look.

103

URBAN
COUNTRY
STYLE

URBAN
COUNTRY
STYLE

ELIZABETH BETTS HICKMAN
and NANCY GENT

Gibbs Smith, Publisher
TO ENRICH AND INSPIRE HUMANKIND

Salt Lake City | Charleston | Santa Fe | Santa Barbara

First Edition
11 10 09 08 07   5 4 3 2 1

Published by
Gibbs Smith, Publisher
P.O. Box 667
Layton, Utah 84041

Orders: 1.800.835.4993
www.gibbs-smith.com

Designed by m:GraphicDesign
Printed and bound in China

Library of Congress Cataloging-in-Publication Data

Hickman, Elizabeth Betts.
  Urban country style / Elizabeth Betts Hickman and Nancy Gent.—1st ed.
      p. cm.
  ISBN-13: 978-1-4236-0159-3
  ISBN-10: 1-4236-0159-9
  1. Interior decoration. I. Gent, Nancy. II. Title.

NK1980.H53 2007
747—dc22
                                        2006031221

dedicated to
Nancy Vera Gent
Liam Vaughn Huber
John L. Hickman
and Sarah F. Zimmerman

contents

acknowledgments

We would like to start with saying that an extraordinary creative friendship brings extraordinary rewards. Like so many great concepts, *Urban-Country Style* began at Nancy Gent's dining room table and has been refined over the last two years to encapsulate what we think is a style that's achievable, a style that crosses age, geographic, and economic boundaries, and a style that brands a new classic. We first want to recognize that it is only with God's love and grace that we are able to accomplish our dreams. Second, we are indebted to our mothers, Vera Gent and Sarah Zimmerman, for their unwavering belief in our abilities, their constant love, and their always impressing upon us that whatever we visualized we could achieve. Connecting early with agent extraordinaire Sorche Fairbank was an auspicious beginning, and we also want to thank photographer Sanford Myers from the bottom of our hearts for his superb work, marvelous sense of humor, and willingness to pitch in to make this book a reality. Finally, we want to thank our publisher, Gibbs Smith, for believing in us.

This book would not have been possible without the initial idea, driving ambition, and focus of Nancy Gent, who has been a delightful person with whom to create a book. Her visual sense brought this project to life. It would also not have been possible without the loving support and technical assistance of my fantastic husband John Hickman, to whom I dedicate the book. I am also indebted to my extraordinary friends, especially Megan Johnson, Jeanne Naujeck, Susan Harlan, Kathy Gray, Dyan Henard, Suzy Kay, and fellow authors Cathy Whitlock and Donna Dorian for always believing in me and listening to me at various times of the day and night as I finished the text and obsessed over details. Thank you, Kevin Coffey, for your architectural advice and friendship. My writing group, which includes fellow writers Jennifer Rechter Paisley and Victoria Hallman, was a tremendous source of encouragement. Likewise my parents and family, especially my incomparable mother Sarah Zimmerman, stylish Mississippi aunt Leita Patton, and cousin Louise Davis, were especially supportive and kind.

Elizabeth Betts Hickman

I would like to thank Elizabeth Hickman for putting words to *Urban-Country Style*. Her extraordinary writing ability, knowledge of design, and sense of humor has made this a cherished experience. To my son Liam, let this book be a testament that anything you put your heart, mind, and soul into can be yours. I love you very much. To Jon Huber, thank you for having faith that I could "make it happen." To Mae Mae, thank you for caring for Liam and me—you are a gem. To my loving brothers and sisters Glenda, Toni, Valerie, Monique, Michael, David, and Sidney and my cousin Pam—thank you for your prayers and encouragement always, and especially over this past difficult year. To my Creative Artists Agency family, particularly Bruce, John, Darin, Jeff H., Charvis, Carrie, Ann, Angie, Toni, and Kim, thank you for your love and support throughout this process and for your steadfast belief that I could bring this book to life. To my extended family: Tom and Wendy, Bill, Kim, Max, and Maggie, thank you for your constant love and support.

Nancy Gent

introduction

Maybe you find yourself drawn to antiques—and to sleek stainless steel appliances. Maybe you like galvanized metal containers *and* smart cotton ticking, or contemporary chairs around an old, traditional farm table. Welcome to urban-country style. Urban-country is a bold new look that's elastic and dynamic, allowing vintage pieces to stand out on their own merit against their contemporary counterparts. Urban-country blends modern understatement and its clean, utilitarian simplicity with the inviting warmth and easy comfort of country style. Its lessons are about focusing on what's important and keeping it close, rather than filling your home with accessories that use space but don't mean anything.

Urban-country isn't about creating a country house in the city, nor is it about creating an urban home in a country setting. It's about combining unexpected materials, such as contemporary lighting and commercial flooring with flea market finds or beloved family furniture, such as your grandmother's simple pine table. Most of us can't or wouldn't start from scratch when revamping our living spaces, and we are therefore faced with using items of different styles, eras, function, and degrees of sentimentality—the latter of which especially comes into play when two households merge into one. Urban-country not only tackles the disparity, it embraces it.

Urban-country is all about FUSION, a modern blend of elements that are

F functional
U unexpected
S simple
I integrated
O old
N new

Why urban-country? Why now? People are scaling back. Simplicity is in, and polishing the silver and dusting the knickknacks is out. We're busy, we're commuting, and we're pulled in different directions. We're also looking for something to connect with, something to speak to us and something that speaks of us, ensconced as we are in a society of mass production. We want to focus on the things that really matter, such as relationships, family, friends, and hobbies.

At the heart of urban-country style is the contrast between old and new, conventional and funky, chic sophistication and cozy comfort. Fashion has already embraced this aesthetic with eclectic combinations such as vintage bouclé Chanel jackets paired with low-rise Seven jeans and ultra-sexy Manolo Blahniks. It's the best blend out there—modern life combined with beloved country style. And we'll show you how to capture it for yourself and your home.

In an urban-country house, items and materials with a modern edge—lamps with drum lampshades, low-voltage halogen spotlights in the ceiling, rubber flooring, neutral walls, and mid-century furniture—look right at home with country furniture, such as a farm table, baskets filled with your child's toys, and maybe an old set of shutters posing as a screen. The urban-country house has wood, metal, a bit of new and old, a little dash of urban sensibility and country stability, and oh, maybe some casters on a table here and there.

The urban-country lifestyle is for folks who don't see themselves in a cold, black leather, stainless steel environment, who aren't in tune with the French-country suburban aesthetic either, and who don't like ultra-fussy traditional style. Urban-country is for everyone who appreciates quality over quantity, has an eye for timeless contemporary classics, and has an admiration for antiques that can breathe in a clean and clear space. It's a livable, modern style for folks looking for relief in a sea of trends and for those trying to focus on spending time with friends and family rather than decorating. Urban-country homes are a mix of items, from the things we bring in, like furniture, to things that may already be there, like faucets or framing. Urban-country style is about creating an integrated environment using our favorite heirlooms alongside fresh, contemporary pieces.

Urban-country style devotees don't mind taking a formal Empire-style mahogany sofa and reupholstering it with soft neutral canvas so it holds up to the uses and rigors of family life (which may include a pet or two). They love limestone or concrete countertops in their kitchen, rubber tile or bleached pine planks on the floor, and a big bowl of apples or grapes on the cocktail table, which just might be a beat-up, flea market find with an interesting new top.

Creating the urban-country lifestyle means clearing the clutter, keeping spaces open and tabletops clear, and keeping what you use close at hand. Sometimes an object you never associated with your house, such as a galvanized metal farm bucket or stock tank, can be mixed into your interiors to provide an inexpensive, durable, and stylish alternative to a more formal piece. This book will show you how something unexpected like this can make your home personal, functional, and, yes, totally hip.

Every person reading this book has a different situation. Maybe you're planning to build a house, thinking of redecorating what you already own, or dreaming about your future home. Perhaps you're simply a design junkie and just love the photographs. Wherever you are on your design journey—and don't think for a moment it's about getting your house "completely finished"—we hope this book will inspire you to achieve it.

Elizabeth and Nancy

FUSION

functional

facing: Designed by Gray Matter
Architecture, this urban-country
style kitchen centers around a
large square island with a metal
base. Above, an industrial-inspired
pot rack hangs from the ceiling near
a steel beam. The abundance of
open shelving, natural light, and
wood cabinetry create a space that's
both functional and aesthetically
beautiful.

Honoring its necessity, function is the first element of urban–country style. Why is function so important? At its very basic level, design cannot succeed without being functional. Your first concern with a house, for instance, should not be how it is decorated but whether it is in satisfactory condition and appropriate for your needs. A fully functional house or apartment meets your needs in both a big-picture way (i.e., with multiple bedrooms if you have

17

children or guests) and on a smaller, more intimate level (a side table and coaster are handy wherever you sit down with a drink).

Bathrooms and kitchens are at the forefront when we think about functional rooms. Without a stove, a kitchen is pretty useless no matter how great its décor. Who cares about wallpaper patterns if you aren't able to cook? While that's an extreme example, too often we get so caught up in redecorating and considering the style of our furnishings that we fail to consider how things really work.

In terms of furniture placement and layout, consider traffic patterns and how the size of your furniture will affect the space. Urban-country style is made for evolution and growth. You don't have to do everything at once—over time you can expand on your basic, most functional needs, such as a sofa, and add the side tables and lamps later. As you live in an environment, you will start to understand what you need to make it complete. For example, you will realize soon enough if you need more seating for your frequent guests, or if a coffee table is sturdy enough to serve as a regular place to prop your feet.

If you have the luxury of planning a new space, think about how you will live there. Mentally bring a load of groceries into your kitchen from the car. Do you have a convenient place on a counter or near the refrigerator to set them? Where does incoming mail go? What if the children or dogs come in wet or muddy?

Pure function is usually too austere for real life. Spaces that are solely functional and nothing more are often cold, plain, and lacking in personality. Think about a hospital room. Sure, someone can sleep there, but it isn't a great model for your bedroom, is it?

Now think about a beautiful, serene space that is simple and unfussy. There aren't piles of

SAVVY URBAN-COUNTRY STYLE TIP: MAKE EVERY CLOSET WORK.

Let's say you have a closet in your guest bedroom that is stuffed with old clothes. Once you have cleared your home of things you don't need—including those clothes you haven't worn in years—consider using that closet for a streamlined office, craft room, or homework space by adding shelving and a desktop cut to fit, and by calling an electrician to add two sockets: one for a lamp and the other for your computer or other electrical equipment. Hall closets can become china cabinets or media storage. Just because a builder calls a space a linen closet, or a previous homeowner used it as one, doesn't mean it has to serve the same purpose for you.

facing: A simple desktop and shelving added to an otherwise unused nook can create a home office, a place to scrapbook, or just a spot to retain your household filing, bills, and recordkeeping.

decorative pillows on the bed that you have to toss off each night, but there are smooth, 100% cotton sheets and a cozy blanket. There aren't a lot of heavy, dust-gathering drapes that need weekly vacuuming, but there are simple shutters that provide privacy and light control and yet can be flung open to let in the morning sun. There aren't many fabrics that bombard you with competing patterns, but there may be two simple armchairs upholstered in a herringbone cotton stripe. The room functions on both an aesthetic and practical level because it's composed of items that are simple, luxurious, and easy to maintain. It has a sense of balance.

Go beyond the ordinary and ready-made. Consider adding casters to your tables, so you can roll them out of the way when you clean or easily move them somewhere else in your home when you're entertaining a crowd. Change the knobs, pulls, and switch plates in your home if they don't excite you. Consider how these everyday items feel in your hand. They are your functional details, after all, and you will deal with them each day, but they don't have to be common.

FUNCTIONAL EXTERIORS AND LANDSCAPING

A sense of balance translates to the exterior of your home, too. If you're planning to build, think about functional choices for your exteriors that will result in minimal maintenance. Fiber-cement planks create a country feel, are impervious to rot, and don't need painting as frequently as clapboards. A true standing-seam metal roof will be more expensive at first, but it will probably outlive you and will never go out of style. Think through your options. Educating yourself about them on the front end of

above: A large mirror on the floor is a time-tested design element that always looks smart and is a great example of how function can be stylish. Pairing creamy white walls with dark furniture is both simple and soothing at the same time.

facing: The large, curtainless, contemporary windows of this Tennessee riverside home designed by Looney Ricks Kiss provide expansive views over the countryside.

a project can potentially save you money, time, and effort in the long term.

What surrounds your house is just as important. For instance, rather than extensive land-scaping, consider garden containers for their low maintenance and stylish qualities, and use plants appropriate for your climate. If you live in an area where temperatures dip below freezing in winter, metal can be a better choice than terra cotta because the former can withstand the elements. Or perhaps consider a lightweight resin planter that can be paint-ed an interesting color.

Instead of the traditional ball-and-cone landscaping surrounding a house, where conical shrubs sit at the corners with tight balls of shrubs in between, think about using gravel all the way up to the foundation. This look, common in Europe, is low maintenance, does not attract pests such as termites, and can lend a crisp quality to the architecture. Another option is to pull the landscaping away from the house to create a zone of low-maintenance plants that complement the house but are still out-of-the-ordinary and unexpected.

KEEPING CHILDREN IN MIND

We have all walked into childproof homes where parents have removed everything at

above, left: If you're building, try to install as much storage as you can. In the Martin home by Nashville-based DA/AD Architects, a playroom area on the second floor is home to a bank of shelves that stash toys and children's games now but could later serve as a very grown-up library or home office space. Note how the shelves are simple—there is no fussy, expensive carving or trim.

above, right: Simple striped and solid cotton fabric bins on wire frames are readily available at many retailers (these came from Bed, Bath and Beyond) and can help keep your closet or shelves neat because they contain the kinds of small items that contribute to a cluttered look.

child level and padded down all hard edges, leaving the space looking unfinished and uninviting. Function *can* be taken too far. Urban-country style is an uncomplicated look that's safe and welcoming for children without forsaking style and personality.

Keep in mind that having children as part of your family can enhance the design process, not limit it. It is a time to consider injecting joyful color and scaling back on furniture to allow more room for a play area, especially in small spaces.

CREATING MULTIFUNCTIONAL SPACES

Losing a seldom-used guest room or a cluttered home office in order to make room for baby gives an opportunity for other rooms to serve dual purposes. It is important to think broadly about multifunctional spaces, since they are the reality for most of us (especially for

above: If you need to create a space for baby and can't knock down a wall, consider "walling" off the space with a pretty, sheer curtain. Note the creative hanging solution for the clothes to the left of the picture: simple pegs hung on the wall take the place of a closet.

SAVVY URBAN-COUNTRY STYLE TIP:
THERE IS NO SUCH THING AS THE FLOOR PLAN POLICE.

Break expected patterns if it suits your situation and makes your home function better. If you do not need a formal dining room, consider using it as an office or a location for the family computer. Or, add bookshelves and a few comfortable chairs and use it as a library. Usually, the dining room is near the kitchen, so the former can become a wonderful spot to create a playroom for a few years while children are young. It can always be transformed back into a dining room later if you change your mind or if you sell your home. In brief, if an unorthodox arrangement of rooms or furnishings works better for you and your family, go for it—and don't worry about it.

above: Creating an organized home is a strong tenet of urban-country style. Here, a simple, functional, L-shaped unit stores coats and boots in style while also serving as a room divider. The open-plan concept may be reminiscent of urban lofts, but the wood and slate materials reference the country. Designed by Alchemy Architects.

facing: Soaring open shelves are an efficient way to make the most of vertical space. Here, an office and reading nook is tucked alongside a hallway, and the open shelves keep the room from feeling too claustrophobic. Designed by LOCUS Architecture.

those in apartments). For example, adding large bookshelves to a wall and running a dining table perpendicular to them can create a space for dining as well as an office space, as long as the supplies are stylishly stashed. Attractive woven baskets or metal bins can help keep the wall organized and clutter free.

If your living room needs to double as a guest room, consider a lightweight futon rather than a pullout sofa bed, a piece that is so often neither a good sofa nor a good bed. Sofa beds are cumbersome, and the cushions that are removed when the sofa becomes a bed take up floor space. Altogether, a futon may be the better choice. And if you still choose to go with a sofa bed, don't skimp on price—spend the money for a premium one.

Consider alternatives to standard chairs, too. Beanbags make for fun seating, especially for children, and they can also be stacked in a corner when not in use. The key is to evaluate how you truly use each room in your home. Be open to changes. If you always pay bills at the same time you watch TV in the family room, consider putting your desk or a small table fitted with desk supplies in the family room. Even if you have a separate room that's designated as a home office, you don't have to use it as such.

KITCHEN CONSIDERATIONS

Kitchens should define functional style. In addition, the kitchen is a great place to take advantage of the many industrial products that lend fun and innovative touches to an urban-country environment. With ever-functional materials such as woods, concrete products for counters or floors, rubber flooring options, and metals for appliances, sinks, counters or backsplashes, the possible combinations are endless. The key is to create a space that affords optimal function and organization, while being keenly stylish at the same time. This does not mean the space needs to be big. It just means you should consider your needs and design accordingly.

Look at your counters and determine what you can put away in drawers or cabinets. If possible, limit countertop items to what you use daily—a coffeemaker, soap, paper towels, or a bowl of fresh fruit. With well-organized cupboards, items are easily accessible, so keeping your counters clear shouldn't be inconvenient. Fewer items on your countertop also means quicker cleanup.

MAKE CHOICES FOR SIMPLER LIVING

Remember that it is a choice to have functional furniture that is easy to clean and easy to move around your home. A slipcovered armchair could work in your living room now and the bedroom of your home in ten years. A leather sofa never goes out of style. Old furniture can be covered with modern fabrics. Metal chairs take a lot of abuse and can work

facing: An overall view of the kitchen in the riverside house shows how simplicity and function come together in an urban-country style kitchen. Since this house is not occupied full-time, the smaller sink and stove make the most of the space, while there is still plenty of storage. Black paint distinguishes the island. Note how the softly painted stair wall works with the pine planks of the kitchen walls.

above, left: A petite model of an Aga—England's fabled cooker known for its vintage looks and high-tech function—nestles beside contemporary cabinets with easy-to-grip metal pulls. Simple, wide pine planks on the backsplash combine beautifully with the stainless-steel hood.

above, right: The best urban-country houses maximize storage. Here, a portion of otherwise-wasted space under the staircase has been carved out to serve as a simple, functional coffee bar, complete with attractive open storage both above and below the countertop.

indoors or outside. You can always add simple, plain cushions for extra comfort and a splash of color.

A lot of home decorating books make a big to-do about accessories. This book is not one of them. Accessories are not part of the urban-country style mix unless they really mean something, like a rock or shell you found on vacation, a favorite book, a lovely picture, or a special gift. Clutter and bric-a-brac is hard on the eyes and is usually high maintenance (think about dust). Remember that an essential benefit of adopting urban-country style is that it makes your life a whole lot easier.

Make a decision to get rid of what you do not use and do not really want. Never an easy choice, of course, but why spend money storing items you never use, or worse, keep tripping around these things in your home? One of the biggest things you can do to make your living space function better immediately is to de-clutter and then evaluate what you have in your rooms. And it doesn't cost a dime.

Too often, we get frustrated trying to put too many pieces of furniture in a room. The solution is not always to seek a larger space. The solution, rather, is to use what you most want, or to make a plan to purchase what you need, and get rid of the rest. Choose to keep details and things with texture, things with a history you know or can easily imagine, and things that are useful, especially those that store other items. Remember too, that overscale, oversized pieces of furniture are made for large homes with large rooms. Forget the notion that they will make everything seem bigger; they will only make your apartment or modest space seem smaller and more cramped.

Think about ways to eliminate unnecessary furniture. Drawers added to custom closets eliminate the need for a chest or additional storage in a bedroom. If you are on a do-it-

facing: Thoughtful storage options, like this bank of wood shelves designed by DuCharme Architecture and tucked in a corner, are a strong component of urban-country style interiors. Look for extra storage wherever you can.

FUNCTIONAL—WHAT REALLY MATTERS

- Whether building, remodeling, or just redecorating, think about yourself and your family, not a fictional future buyer.
- Factor in the time spent cleaning when you're making design decisions. A pleated lampshade, for instance, will gather more dust than a simple drum shade.
- Don't be intimidated by someone else's expectations of what rooms you should have in your home.
- It doesn't matter how great something looks if it doesn't work for the way you live.
- A functional house is easier to clean, looks better, and will make you happier.

left: A groove cut around the edge of this integrated concrete sink and counter means that custom cutting boards can be used for food preparation or to cover the sink to provide a broad work surface if needed. Designed by LOCUS Architecture.

facing: A large, restaurant-style faucet serves the length of the sink and looks sculptural in its own right.

yourself budget, rework your own closets with ready-made organizing components, and put a small chest of drawers in a closet to maximize your floor space. All you really need are a bed, end tables, and good lighting in a bedroom.

A functional approach to design is the key toward creating a space that is easy to care for and easy to live with, and that makes you, your family, and your guests comfortable. ▮

facing: Sliding translucent panels reveal a functional closet and a dresser that appears both vintage and updated at the same time. Cool concrete floors are perfect underfoot in a Texas house.

right: Simple and beautiful: A wrought-iron railing marches up the staircase in this riverside house in Tennessee. Note, too, how the space is illuminated by ceiling-mounted halogen fixtures, and drawers are cut into the side of the staircase to maximize storage.

unexpected

facing: Designed by Scooter J. Construction, this classic urban-country style cottage in Nashville includes unexpected elements, like orange chairs paired with a vintage metal table, and simple forms, like the gabled roof and traditional windows. Galvanized, corrugated steel siding lends an urban feel that also references old farm sheds. An easygoing connection between the indoors and outdoors doubles the living space.

All too often, interiors are far too expected and predictable, such as the standard, oversized brown leather sofa accompanied by a brown coffee table and plain armchairs upholstered in a tan chenille fabric. Urban-country style embraces the unexpected because at its heart is contrast through elements you often can't just go buy at the store. The inclusion of opposites is automatically attractive, definitely unexpected, and never boring.

above: A juicy red hue and clever inversion distinguishes this barn-like home, which reveals its sophistication on closer inspection. Designed by Alchemy Architects, it combines a simple, traditional shape and color with urban windows and a metal roof. Be aware that there are different types of metal roofing. The least expensive is known as "5V" or barn metal roofing, which is applied with visible fasteners. Standing seam metal roofs are more expensive but last the longest.

facing: This California home by DuCharme Architecture pairs an urban-inspired concrete wall with a rustic, copper-clad door and warm hardwood floors.

SAVVY URBAN-COUNTRY STYLE TIP:
THE ANSWER MAY BE INDUSTRIAL.

Rather than be limited by the hooks and railings available in home-improvement, hardware, and decorating stores, why not look at industrial options with a fresh eye? Plumbing pipe can be cut to any length and provides an instant, industrial update for a fraction of the cost of fancier stair railings or towel racks. The cool reward? You can customize your house for less than you'd pay for off-the-rack railings.

above: It's a factory . . . it's a barn . . . it's an urban-country style home. Lake/Flato Architects of Texas converted this renovated industrial building, whose shape is reminiscent of a barn, into a sophisticated home.

Your home doesn't have to look like everyone else's home, all of your furnishings don't have to come from the same place, and you don't even have to use your rooms in the same way as your neighbors. Urban-country style is about considering some basic questions: how you *really* live, what you *really* need, and how to achieve it with real-life resources (meaning without a million-dollar inheritance).

Think beyond the usual when it comes to your home. What about using sliding hardware tracks, like the kind used for barn doors, to mount your interior doors? This choice saves space (especially in a tight area), is an economic alternative to built-in pocket doors, and is also visually appealing. Why not use chain-link fencing (what could be more urban?) in a wood frame to safely encase your deck instead of using the predictable all-wood railing? Chain-link is interesting and funky, allows optimal views from a deck, and costs less than finished wood.

CONNECT THE UNEXPECTED

Two different influences are at work in a sleek kitchen with stainless appliances, limestone countertops, and a big, country-style farm table used as an island. There is a strong country element, of course, but a strong urban component as well, and the unexpected combination looks great. Likewise, an antique bed you inherited looks updated and interesting when dressed in contemporary bedding and flanked with modern halogen sconces that provide excellent light for bedtime reading.

above: Just because you have an old house doesn't mean you have to find accessories that match the same era. Another tip: If your fireplace isn't operable, consider stacking a group of sturdy votives for a romantic glow.

If you're in an apartment or if remodeling is not feasible, there are still some easy tips you can initiate to change your plain, predictable backdrop. Consider taking down the chandelier in the dining area and installing a clean-lined fixture with a big drum shade. (Just make sure you keep the original fixture to re-install before you move.) In the bathroom, use a tension rod placed an inch or two from the ceiling to hang a long curtain panel—consider plain burlap or a crisp length of cotton ticking—to cover a shower door or to cover a lower tension rod with a plastic shower curtain liner. The height of the fabric panel will draw the eye upward and make the bath seem larger and more luxurious. Since most apartments have a big, plain mirror above the sink, consider hanging an old mirror, framed with barn wood, with fishing line on a screw set into the wall above the existing mirror.

facing: This sleek, urban-country style kitchen designed by Nashville-based Rozanne Jackson stars a 16-foot, turn-of-the century French textile table.

above, left: In this house designed by Alchemy Architects, the unexpected solution of plank doors on hardware normally seen on overhead garage doors adds style and saves space in this bedroom. Built-in shelving tucks under the eaves and is another space-saving trick.

above, right: Something readymade, like an old dress form, can become a piece of sculpture. Look for things with personal meaning, and celebrate them.

These little changes can go a long way in adding a sophisticated urban-country feel to your vanilla-walled, vanilla-carpeted space. What you choose to use or display in a particular room should be personal and ideally go beyond the expected. If your backdrop is plain and predictable, there's no reason everything has to be that way. Look for things in your possession that are simply sentimental or personally special. For example, if your grandmother was a seamstress and you have an old dress form that she used, by all means "use" it yourself in your bedroom or a guest room. View it with a fresh perspective, and allow it to stand on its own so you can appreciate its shape and history. You don't have to use it as a valet and pile it with clothes. Something that was once purely functional can become a focal point that serves as unexpected sculpture.

CREATE YOUR OWN EXPECTATIONS

What do you expect when you go inside a home? The dining room has to have a table and chairs, the bedroom has to have a matching "suite" of a bed, dresser, and tall chest—or so we have been trained to believe. You've seen this philosophy time and again in magazines and advertising, and you may have heard it from builders, realtors, designers, or even your mother.

Indeed, you may need a dining room if you entertain a large family several times a year. However, if you are fond of casual outdoor buffets, maybe that square footage that is now devoted to a dining room can be used in a different way, and your outdoor space can benefit from some extra attention. If you are in a one-bedroom apartment and you find yourself needing a nursery or an office, consider "walling off" the dining room with curtains hung on simple metal wire or a long tension rod.

On a macro level, personalizing your space means decorating for yourself and not for some undefined future buyer who may purchase your house someday. Paint is a cheap, easy, low-impact way to change a room, so letting your daughter have the fuchsia room she really wants is not going to impact the resale value of your house.

On a micro level, this means having a yard sale or a swap meet with friends or getting on the Internet and selling anything that you bought just to fill a space. You don't have to spend money on fake plants above your kitchen cabinets simply because it seems bare. It's best to let your home evolve over time—why rush? Instead of those fake plants in the kitchen, give that dead space above the cabinets a good cleaning and leave it empty, or

right: Think about the unexpected: Here, a lineup of different chairs can easily be pulled up to the old wooden table in this home designed by Vicente Wolf.

use containers to store things you need less frequently. When you get the chance to build or remodel, vow to specify cabinets that go to the ceiling. Consider leaving the space above your fireplace bare until you find the right object. One day you'll find the perfect work of art, or even a piece of ironwork. You could even use something like your grandmother's old garden gate or a section of new picket fence. Perhaps painting the fireplace wall a color or texture that stands on its own as a focal point will be more satisfying. Why not defy the expected choices?

DESIGN YOUR OWN DETAILS

Keeping things clean and contemporary without starting from scratch is a major factor to keep in mind as you take a critical look at your home, apartment, or a potential new decorating or renovation plan. The elements that make your home different from everyone else's home should be unexpected. You want to be surprised, delighted, and happy when you step inside, not feel like you've entered a far-flung branch of a store or catalog. The best houses have interesting textures and elements in them, such as a huge shell found at the beach and now used as a doorstop, a handsome old table made by a grandfather, or a wonderful photograph enlarged and framed as art in a hall.

Speaking of art, consider creating your own. Donate those cheap posters and prints that still lurk in your home or in your closets; instead, enlarge some of your favorite photos—or just one—and you will have a completely personalized piece of art. If you use multiple photos, try to frame them alike for simplicity and ease of arrangement. With today's digital technology, color photos can become black-and-white at the touch of a button, and you can even enlarge just one face or one portion of a photograph. Go beyond portraits, too. Consider a series of flower shots from your garden, photos of sporting pursuits, or pictures of your pet. Another idea is to use old family photos to bring a sense of the personal past into your home.

facing, top left: Chalkboard panels are yet another candidate for overhead sliding tracks. What could be more fun covering your child's closet?

facing, top right: Art doesn't have to come from a gallery. Hanging a grouping—whether it's your child's work, photographs you've taken over the years, or vintage photos from your family—is a dramatic way to make a collection of small things really stand out and create a focal point.

facing, bottom: Innovative ideas for a more functional home:
- Built-in storage. Low cubbies keep books close at hand. When items have their own home, countertops and the dining room table won't become de facto desks. Designed by LOCUS Architecture.
- Ready-made art. A wall coated with chalkboard paint means that messages and grocery lists are handy, and that everyone can have some art on view.

SAVVY URBAN-COUNTRY STYLE TIP:
THE RESTAURANT SUPPLY STORE CAN YIELD THE UNEXPECTED:

- Rustproof metal baking sheets in different sizes to corral boots and shoes on the floor of your mudroom, or to use as resilient trays for outdoor entertaining.
- Simple, durable white china for less than you would spend at a specialty store.
- Dimpled, stainless steel bread pans that can be used to organize drawers, contain stationery and office supplies on your desktop, or hold a variety of small presents as part of a gift.

left: A soft blue urban-country style living room in this Nashville apartment has the ultimate unexpected country coffee table: an overturned stock tank bought at a farm supply store. It's the perfect height and depth, and it's practically indestructible—if it can handle cows in a field, it can handle your guests!

You might consider such details as using an old country kitchen sink—the shallow kind with big porcelain drain boards on either side—as a clever focal point for a large powder room, or using outdoor lighting inside your home, or reworking an industrial artifact into a piece of furniture.

UNEXPECTED MATERIALS AND SOURCES

If you're fortunate enough to be building or remodeling, unexpected materials make all the difference in an urban-country house. Galvanized, corrugated steel can wrap around a bar, island, or bath surround. Plumbing pipe can create a towel holder or the framework for a table or bed. Glass garage doors used in place of windows can be flung open to create a romantic indoor-outdoor room that's perfect for entertaining. And why not add an outdoor shower to use all summer?

right: Simple, chic, and inexpensive: Galvanized outdoor fixtures like this one are widely available in two sizes at home improvement stores, and are very affordable alternatives to other types of indoor fixtures.

left: A standard-sized glass garage door is an unexpected and yet completely functional addition to this end of an eat-in kitchen designed by Nashville-based designer Beth Haley. The door takes up the same amount of space as three French doors, yet costs less and lends a far more unique style. A screen tucks up out of sight yet can be pulled down to make the kitchen feel like a screened porch.

facing, left: Use color sparingly to make an impression that you won't tire of over time. Here, a saturated lavender hue was used for a back entry hall. Note how the bedroom to the right is simple, unfussy, and clad in soft neutrals. Outside, gravel is laid up to the edge of the house in order to provide a chic, low-maintenance ground cover that also provides for excellent drainage. Designed by LOCUS Architecture.

facing, right: The unexpected addition of an interior window and a bright blue color on the walls enlivens this corridor, which includes plenty of natural wood.

left: Tennessee-based architect Kevin Coffey designed the Johnson home, which is located on a working horse farm, to reference familiar farmhouses but also provide a contemporary, functional space for a growing family. The lively pattern of windows on the west side of the house shows how new and old influences can work together.

facing: In this country home designed by Tennessee-based Kennon Taylor Architects, a custom steel stair railing created from commercial beams provides a swooping focal point in a sunny living room. The urban element is set off with warm wood flooring and a wood-paneled ceiling.

Color, too, can be a big part of an unexpected experience when it comes to your home. By painting your exterior or even just your front door an unexpected color, you will inject a sense of energy. Shapes can also be unexpected. For instance, you may decide to have a circular island in your kitchen or an unusual chair by your front door.

If you are lucky enough to be working with an architect, the home's shape can provide an unexpected infusion of energy. Maybe that energy comes from an overscaled dormer, a lively pattern of windows on the side of the house, or a dramatic urban detail, like a stair railing that resembles an industrial beam.

top: The opposite side of this home by Gray Matter Architecture shows a massing of elements that immediately identify it as a contemporary structure, but the wood framed windows and barn door sneak in as country-inspired touches. The planting bed of simple green reeds and the lack of fussy foundation plants are tenets of urban-country style landscaping.

bottom: A closer look at this urban home by Gray Matter Architecture reveals country elements in the wood-trimmed windows, angled shed roof, and sliding barn-like doors that open the home to the outdoors.

above, left: Mixing materials is key when it comes to creating an urban country look, whether it's an exterior or an interior. Here, vivid red planks on this Minnesota house, designed by Minneapolis-based LOCUS Architecture, contrast with the rustic stone and sleek windows.

right: An expected shape—a gable roof—is paired with an unexpectedly oversized dormer on this home designed by LOCUS Architecture. There is a sense of the familiar and the fresh in the asymmetrical pattern of windows and the generous use of stone.

How you use materials, too, makes a difference. Glossy, dark walnut planks laid on the diagonal make for an interesting riff on the traditional hardwood floor, while industrial-scale windows and doors can flood a home with amounts of sunlight and air that are just not possible with the expected residential-scale options.

Be brave. The unexpected, by definition, requires imagination and boldness. Investigate the artisans in your area (and realize that they may be the guys working at your local auto body shop). Anything metal can be powder coated, which is a durable, painted finish like that on cars. You can use galvanized metal stock tanks from a farm supply store as big planters. A plastics company can create custom ice buckets or trough containers for flowers. Don't overlook your area's metal fabricators—they can create stunning metal shelving or custom furniture, and might be delighted to take on a creative task.

left: Commercial products, like the windows in the Nashville home of designer Rozanne Jackson and husband Glen Oxford, can provide an excellent alternative to standard residential options. Commercial windows and doors typically provide larger expanses of glass and a more contemporary grid pattern than traditional windows.

facing: Think creatively when you're looking for something special. Fabricated by a local plastics company, this beautiful heavyweight, watertight, plastic trough was designed to hold flowers, candles, or small dishes of hors d'oeuvres.

So seek the unexpected, make your home your own, and don't concern yourself with what is "correct" or in style at the moment. If you are only following a fad, then it's bound to be out of style in a few years. That is why it is so critical to avoid trendy paint colors, and every decade has them. (Remember avocado and harvest gold? Mauve and aqua? Navy blue, burgundy, and dark green?)

Don't focus on the expected. Focus on what works for your situation, yourself, and your family, whether you have a six-year-old child or a six-week-old puppy. Or maybe it's just you. You count. Make your house count, too. ▥

UNEXPECTED—WHAT REALLY MATTERS

- Consider commercial alternatives when it comes to windows, doors, and hardware. You'll find them through architectural firms, builders, and building supply companies. You'll also find a more contemporary range of styles, yet the prices may be less than if you commissioned custom designs. A big plus: commercial-grade products are often built to be more durable than their residential-grade counterparts. Still, make sure you compare like products. Commercial alternatives come in a range of quality levels just as residential materials do.
- Don't get caught up with what others will think. Your home is for you, and if you want to do something fun and unexpected, it's to your benefit. Don't be afraid to give it a go.
- Mixing is generally smart, stylish, and cost effective. Think contrast when pairing things, such as inexpensive flea market finds with contemporary clear plastic chairs, or vintage linen kitchen towels reworked into pillows for a clean-lined sofa.

simple

facing: Modern reproductions of classic country pieces, like these Windsor chairs and clean-lined table, serve as beautiful and functional elements in the Martin family's dining room, which features contemporary sconces and gleaming wood floors. The architecture team from Nashville-based firm DA/AD designed the bank of windows—which would look right at home in an urban-high rise—to showcase the view.

U ntil recently, the concept of simplicity had somewhat of a bad reputation. If a home was described as simple, it was code for modest, bare, and plain. Not any more. Simple isn't stark, cold, empty, or austere, either. These days, the word "simple" adorns magazine titles. The concept of an uncomplicated home represents an admirable goal for many people. There is a desire to simplify, clear out the clutter, and create spaces that are streamlined in terms of color and style, which allows for visual continuity and less stress.

URBAN-COUNTRY STYLE: SIMPLE YET LUXURIOUS

The urban-country style home—whether apartment, townhouse, suburban spread, or country farmhouse—is simple in the sense that it's unfussy and practical. Yet it is also elegant in its simplicity. A room may simply contain an Empire-style sofa clad in crisp cotton ticking, clear resin cubes for a cocktail table, a large floor lamp with a bell shade, and an arrangement of black-framed family photos hung against a white wall. This mix is both smart and uncomplicated. Although varying in style, the arrangement is pulled together and works because the pieces stand out and don't compete with each other. Their individual beauty and form can be appreciated, and each piece has a purpose. Everything appears carefully chosen because it is. The furniture is comfortable. The lighting is thoughtfully placed, and the storage is functional. In brief, the house works, and it appears soothing because of its simplicity.

Simple solutions, like using wall ledges to display art or photographs, allow end tables to remain clutter free. There is flexibility because pieces can be switched out and moved around without the hassles of a nail and hammer.

PRACTICAL CONSIDERATIONS

When it comes to the biggest piece of furniture in your living room, leather or slipcovered sofas are the best for comfort and for standing up to heavy use. Striped fabrics, especially ticking, checks, and solids, are favorite urban-country choices for sofas, chairs, beanbags, and pillows. But you won't see any ruffles or

above: Urban-country homes are innately unpretentious and functional. On this house designed by Alchemy Architects, a simple wooden platform serves as an oversized welcome mat, and a handy bench is thoughtfully placed near the door. The gravel bed against the house makes sense for drainage since this side of the house doesn't have gutters. It also cuts down on time spent on yard work.

facing: Janus et Cie's Kenton chairs gather around a wooden table with an iron base in this eating area, which features a bank of closed storage behind smooth panels.

facing: Warm wooden floors and bookcases, a handsome yet simple stone fireplace, and steel cables create an urban-country atmosphere in this home, which feels serene because it isn't cluttered. A simple yet meaningful picture—not a mantel "styled" with bland, meaningless accessories—sets off the wood-burning fireplace. Designed by Lake/Flato Architects.

this page: In this Texas house, an urban-inspired sink in the guest room is a riff on the old-fashioned country washstand.

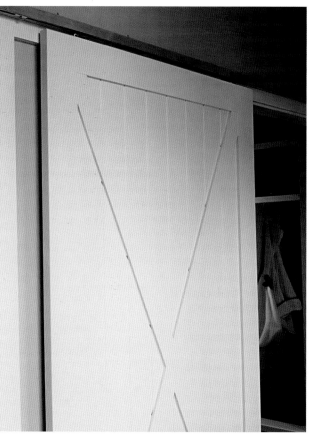

thick flanges. Prints, too, are typically kept to a minimum in favor of fresh stripes and checks. You won't see any chintz. The country elements of urban-country style are honest, simple, and plain, never cutesy or fluffy.

In furnishing your living room, make sure your rug is large enough—and that means large enough so that every piece of furniture in the seating group has all four feet on the rug (although you can get away with only the front feet of a sofa on the rug). When you're selecting a rug, remember to go for solid colors and soft finishes. Sisal or seagrass are inexpensive options for adding texture. However, if you have small children, you might want to choose a wool version for its durability, comfort, and easy-to-clean properties.

If you choose to hang art on the wall rather than display

facing, top left: Exposed hardware comes in a variety of styles and provides visual interest as well as pure function.

facing, top right: Sliding tracks can be used to mount any type of door. In the Martin house, which was designed by Nashville architecture firm DA/AD, a barn-style door is hung on a track and reveals (or hides, if necessary) an expansive mudroom with slate floors and plenty of cubbies.

facing, bottom: A simple, pine-framed French door slides on an overhead galvanized track (a stock item that can be found at farm stores and cut to any length) and serves as a clever divider between a kitchen and living room.

this page: Swing-arm lamps keep the bedside table clear in this simply-appointed bedroom, which includes a bed that was designed and made by Nashville homeowner Andy Roddick (no, not the tennis player). The wonderful, ethnic textile on the bed was a gift from a family member.

left: An urban-style metal ceiling fan cools a guest room that's an update on the simple bunkhouse, complete with a country cowhide and striped blankets.

them on ledges, keep some basic rules in mind. The primary rule is not to hang anything too high. Maintain only about six inches of space from the bottom of the frame to the top of your sofa. If you're hanging art in a corridor or on its own, keep things at eye level (never higher than your forehead).

A major advantage to keeping your style simple is that when a similar philosophy is applied to almost anything, be it materials, furnishings, fabrics, or layouts, things tend to work better. In general terms, simpler options may cost less, be easier to clean, and make more sense for families with children or pets. And keeping things simple at home means more time for your hobbies, your family, your interests, and, in general, your life.

SAVVY URBAN-COUNTRY STYLE TIP:
AVOID USELESS EXTRAS.

If you find yourself tossing pillows on the floor every night before you go to sleep, do yourself and your partner a favor and simplify your bedroom by tossing those throw pillows permanently. Another bonus: less fabric means fewer harbors for nasty dust mites, plus less cleaning.

When it comes to getting rid of other "extras," remember that donating things you don't need might net you a tax break, and it makes your house function better. You won't spend as much time searching for items or trying to come up with ways to store things. However, if the item in question has been in your family, do the right thing and offer it to other family members first before you sell or donate.

SAVVY URBAN-COUNTRY STYLE TIP:
CHOOSE QUALITY OVER QUANTITY.

Don't skimp on your bedding—it is something you touch every day. Buy the highest quality 100% cotton or linen sheeting you can with a minimum 200 thread count (a higher thread count means softer, long-lasting bed linens). Apply this axiom throughout your home: if it's something you use or touch daily (such as a knob in your kitchen), make sure it is as perfect as you can find and afford.

facing: For a restful setting conducive to sleep, make your bed with only the pillows and linens you truly use. Urban-country style bedrooms don't include fussy, seldom-washed comforters or decorative pillows.

SAVVY URBAN-COUNTRY STYLE TIP: *IF YOU'RE BUILDING, KEEP IT SIMPLE.*

- Think about your layout and how you really live. If you never entertain formally, you may not need a dining room. Consider a combination library/office instead, or an open floor plan with an eat-in kitchen.

- A simple plan is easier to build and costs less. Do you really need five different roof levels and multiple gables? Simplifying the roofline as well as the "footprint" of a house can also result in a cost savings. For example, a house that is mostly a rectangle is less expensive to build than one with lots of curves or "bump-outs." And a complicated roofline isn't only more expensive to build; it's also more expensive to repair and, eventually, replace.

- Do you really need an extra-large "garden" tub? So many homeowners rarely use these expensive tubs, and they take up a lot of space. If you would like a tub, consider purchasing a claw-foot version from an architectural salvage company and having it reglazed, or simply buying a new version.

- Consider the flow of air when you evaluate a plan; whether it is a stock plan provided by a builder or a magazine, or one that is custom designed by an architect, think what screened windows and doors you could open for air flow on a crisp fall day.

above: Halls and passageways of any kind are wonderful spots for shelves, cubbies, or any type of storage. With an abundance of natural light and air from the windows that open along this corridor, this home designed by Gray Matter Architecture has a lovely open, airy feeling. Note the interesting contemporary-style sconces, which direct light down toward the floor.

facing: The simple lines of the wood and metal in the stairwell of this home, designed by DuCharme Architecture, show just how nicely these classic country and urban materials work together.

above: Classic wicker pieces from California-based design company Janus et Cie anchor this serene living room, which is sophisticated and urbane, yet as comfortable as a screened porch in the country.

facing: Serenity is an urban-country living room: the wool sisal carpet is soft and easy-to-clean, the comfortable chair wears a canvas slipcover, and simple painted panels streamline the built-in shelves. An easy idea for a long-lasting fresh arrangement: Look for inexpensive bunches of bear grass, like the clumps seen here on the mantel, and place them in tall glass containers with water and simple black river rocks.

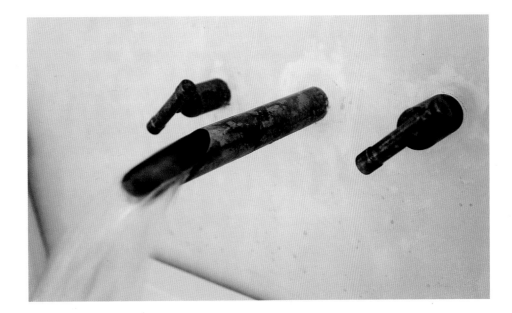

above: Instead of running through a store-bought faucet, the water in this Texas home flows out through a simple pipe cut on an angle with honed edges. The hot and cold taps, also created from plumbing pipe, have the same lovely patina.

facing: Painting one wall in a room can add color and interest without a big commitment.

SIMPLE—WHAT REALLY MATTERS

- Simple silhouettes don't go out of style as quickly as trendy pieces of furniture or accessories.
- Think quality over quantity in every aspect of your home.
- A tried-and-true design tip that's worth repeating: If you love color, buy it in an accessory, like a box or lampshade, rather than investing in a piece of furniture. If you're interested in a vivid wall color, try it in a powder room or a guest room, where you can enjoy it without it overpowering your home.
- Keep it classic: consider choosing plain white towels, sheets, toilet paper, and paper towels. There's a reason that's all you see at the finest, most luxurious hotels.

this page: Warm neutral walls, soft white slipcovers, and cabinetry unify an integrated kitchen/living/dining area in this home. An open plan is an urban concept, while the stove in the corner is clearly a country element. Designed by Alchemy Architects.

facing: A peek through a country-inspired door reveals a peaceful urban-country style bedroom without a lot of fuss and fluff.

left: A transparent glass shower door makes the most of the space in this bath. If you're in a rental, consider a clear plastic shower curtain hung as close to the ceiling as you can, or choose cotton canvas or ticking. Designed by DuCharme Architecture.

facing: Gleaming wood floors, luminous glass tile, and custom vanities with large sinks and plenty of storage anchor this spacious bath, designed by DuCharme Architecture, which features a modern take on the claw-foot tub. Note the abundance of fresh white linens, which are classic, simple, and serene.

integrated

In urban-country style spaces, there is an integration of practical and beautiful, and a balance between contemporary chic and country charm. When you're evaluating your rooms, remember to balance urban elements, such as modern chairs or metal tables, with country elements, such as an antique table, a piece of white ironstone dinnerware, or a stack of comfortable quilts.

Keeping the concept of balance in mind as you approach the decorating or building process may be helpful, especially as you work around things you cannot change. It's also important to literally keep things balanced, from light distributed evenly throughout a room to having balanced seating to making sure all of your furniture isn't too heavily weighted to one side of the space.

Why is it important to think about integrating everything in our homes when it comes to design? It is because most of the time, we are working around something that we cannot move or replace at the moment. The object you are working around might be a white laminate countertop in your kitchen that you cannot afford to rip out and replace right now, or a roomful of furniture you inherited and are not going to sell. Whatever it is (and most of us have something that falls into this category), it is important to work in what we love with what we have to live with, even if it is temporary. You might be integrating your furniture and possessions with someone else's, or you might be starting fresh and integrating some new things in with a few beloved pieces you've had all of your life. The key is to make everything work together.

STYLE WITHOUT BOUNDARIES

Indeed, urban-country is a truly integrated look because it functions for everyone. The six elements of the style—functional, unexpected, simple, integrated,

facing: Beams, stone walls, and a rustic table are classic country elements in this sophisticated California kitchen by DuCharme Architecture, which features three layers of lighting (the central candle-like chandelier, the recessed lighting, and the pendants over the sink). The urban materials—steel, polished granite, and glass—are highlighted by the soft gray "floating" cabinetry against the window, and a wonderful old wooden table.

facing: This home mixes wood, glass, and concrete for a friendly, approachable take on contemporary-flavored urban-country style. Note how the simple steps connect the lawn with the outdoor living area. Designed by DuCharme Architecture.

above: Franklin, Tennessee-based architect Kevin Coffey designed his own residence to feel right at home in the woods. With a rich palette of unexpected color, the house has the vertical feel of urban homes with the visual appeal of a simple farmhouse.

left: Another view of the kitchen in this California home designed by Gray Matter Architecture showcases the staircase, which is composed of thick steps paired with metal cables, supports, and railings.

above: Ultimate urban-country:
This bathroom, designed by
Alchemy Architects, features a
veritable checklist of urban-country
style features, from the corrugated
wainscoting that wraps the lower
walls; the functional, commercial-
style faucet and taps; the
wood-trimmed vanity mirror and
storage that recalls old houses;
and the industrial-inspired housing
for the plain white china sink.

old, and new—naturally lend themselves to universal design, which is the fancy design-world way of saying "design for everyone": young and old, able-bodied and not. For example, a wide doorway is easier, whether you are carrying groceries into your house, maneuvering a walker, leading your big dogs outdoors, or holding your twins on your hips while moving to another room. Likewise a walk-in shower: easier for someone maneuvering a wheelchair, but also great for bathing those big dogs or cleaning a clutch of kids after a painting party or a day in the sandbox. In brief, do not just integrate old and new, urban and country—truly work in elements that make your house comfortable for anyone.

INTEGRATED EXTERIORS

The idea of an integrated style is natural when it comes to thinking about the exteriors of our homes. What do you picture when you think of buildings in the country? Materials like barn wood, stone, clapboard planks, corrugated metal, and wood shingles probably come to mind. What are many urban buildings created from? Glass, stainless steel, brick, and cut-and-polished stone.

Urban-country style exteriors marry materials. Maybe it is a stone cottage with a corrugated metal addition. Maybe it is a modern, steel-framed house filled with wonderful old, wide-plank wood floors and ceilings rescued from a tobacco barn. In either case, the materials cooperate because they are honest, they are durable, and through their contrast, they complement one another.

Exteriors that showcase the urban-country style aesthetic might lean more toward country or urban, depending on their setting and their designers. It is not so much about the materials; it is rather how the materials are used. A house might be completely glass and steel, yet be filled with fine American antiques set off by

left: Consider a commercial-style, ceiling-mounted track for a shower curtain instead of the expected, wall-mounted tension rod, and your ceiling will look taller. Another urban-country style tip: Exchange your showerhead and all faucets for modern-looking fixtures in silver tones, and banish any brass finishes.

facing: Designed by Nancy Gent in a circa 1928 cottage, this renovated bath has integrated and simple features:

- Industrial elements, like the beaker-style light fixture, are paired with classic fittings such as the bathtub and sink, which were re-glazed a snowy white.
- A standard 4" white field tile blends with a slight splurge—a "rug" designed from more-expensive glass and stainless metal tiles.
- In an east-facing room, translucent glass allows maximum light but maintains privacy without the need for curtains or blinds.

SAVVY URBAN-COUNTRY STYLE TIP:
A VINTAGE BATH CAN GET AN URBAN-COUNTRY MAKEOVER.

- Consider using a ceiling-mounted track for a shower curtain. Not only will there be no unsightly bar, but also your ceilings will look taller.
- Exchange your showerhead and all faucets for more modern-looking stainless fixtures. Banish brass finishes.
- Remove your overhead lighting fixture and replace it with one that has more pizzazz, or consider adding clean-lined sconces on either side of the mirror.
- Replace vintage doors caked with old paint with doors in natural wood finishes, or consider using doors with opaque, sandblasted, or heavy ribbed glass. If you're interested in keeping an old door, clean, strip, and repaint it.
- Use simple, silver-finish metal levers or plain knobs on doors and cabinetry; don't choose excessively decorative hardware.

a richly stained concrete floor. Industrial, metal-mesh shelving might showcase old books, while a steel cube might sport a Shaker-style wooden tray as a cocktail table.

A good rule of thumb with urban-country exteriors is to make sure the integration of materials makes sense. Wood and metal are obvious bedfellows because one sees these materials all over the countryside and in the city. Stone and stainless might seem more of a stretch, but not when one thinks about the fact that treated metal (often with a rust-resistant coating) is so often used for roofing on barns in the countryside. Make sure you consult with your builder or architect, however, if you are considering some unorthodox combinations. Some types of metal roofing, for instance, are not compatible. It's critical that you solicit professional advice.

If you have a choice, think twice about using brick. An urban-country exterior typically is not brick, unless it is paired with metal columns rather than composite or wood choices, and the roofing and detailing clearly reference contemporary elements. Generally, brick automatically lends a formal, suburban, traditional look to new homes, but there are exceptions, of course, such as a brick-and-stone cottage kitted out with cool metal window boxes or contemporary planters. Of course, if you have brick, consider painting it a fresh, creamy white to create a calming background. Various stucco finishes, too, can completely change the look of a brick home and transform it into a more contemporary-looking home.

Concrete, stone, wood or fiber-cement planks, metal, and tile are all solid components of urban-country style exteriors. Commercial materials, like COR-TEN® steel sheets, often weather beautifully. Drive through the industrial edge of a city if you are planning to build and want to glean some new ideas. Likewise, consider driving through the countryside and paying attention to barns, sheds, and other working buildings. Take photographs and make notes. Open your mind to different possibilities for your home.

SAVVY URBAN-COUNTRY STYLE TIP:
DRUM SHADES=MODERN DRAMA.

Lamps are the forgotten orphans of many rooms, and we tend to hold onto old lampshades until the bitter end. Don't do it. For starters, ripped lampshades or linings can be a fire hazard, and dusty shades, frankly, look terrible. An easy, inexpensive urban-country style update is to find smart new "drum" shades, which are essentially cylinders of fabric, paper, or silk. They'll immediately update any lamp you have. And if your lamp base is scary . . . remember, there's always spray paint (in flat black, not glossy).

facing: Although this glossy-white, 1970s-era ginger-jar lamp is a classic, a simple drum shade provides an instant update.

facing: A functional and stylish urban-country home on a tight city lot is integrated:

- It blends materials. A metal roof lends durability and style, large windows take advantage of sunlight and views, and no-maintenance Plexiglas panels lend a translucent quality.
- It incorporates smart landscaping. Plantings should complement a setting, not dominate it now or in the future. Dwarf varieties of plants and trees won't become overgrown in a few years.
- It takes advantage of its setting. A small lot is an opportunity to go up, not out, and a thoughtful floor plan can be designed for privacy.

right: Log construction is undeniably a country form of building, but when it is paired with contemporary light fixtures, steel railings, and reinforced concrete, it becomes urban-country. Designed by Gray Matter Architecture.

INTEGRATING THE OLD WITH THE NEW IN YOUR INTERIORS

When it comes to your interiors, think about balance and contrast as you work in old and new pieces. Consider pairing clean-lined, squared-off furniture with rustic, wide-plank wood floors; the contrast allows both elements to come into focus. If you go into a house that is all one style, you miss half of everything because it all looks the same, or at the least it looks like something you have seen elsewhere. With proper contrast, each piece stands out and tells a story about who lives with it.

When it comes to your kitchens and bathrooms, which generally contain limited

facing: Integrating natural and manmade materials is a strong component of urban-country style. In this Texas house by architecture firm Lake/Flato, steel, glass, and concrete combine with natural stone to create a house that's stylish yet supremely functional and appropriate for its setting.

right: Minneapolis-based architecture firm LOCUS Architecture combined clapboard siding and a barn-style door on this contemporary pool house. Concrete pavers outlined with turf are a classic urban-country combination when it comes to terraces, pool surrounds, and paths.

facing: At first glance, this house looks completely urban contemporary. But country makes an appearance in the wood, which was applied to the exterior in a tight clapboard pattern, and the landscaping, which is clearly simple and low-maintenance. The house exudes functional, simple style. Designed by LOCUS Architecture.

right: Stylish wooden folding chairs and wood planks on the floor and ceiling bring a country sensibility to this otherwise contemporary dining area, which features a soaring ceiling, discreet sconces, and an urban-inspired table. Designed by LOCUS Architecture.

amounts of furniture but many built-in elements, do not forget that they need the same focused attention in terms of style and integration. For instance, wood, glass, and stainless steel can set off much-loved and much-expected tile. While remaining basic and practical, the mix will add interesting detail. Even simple ideas, like nailing buckets to the wall from their base to create "tubes" of storage for towels or toiletries, or using pipes for your towel bars, make your home distinctive. Another advantage to these types of imaginative, *integrated* design ideas is that these solutions are readily available in the form of items you can buy at hardware, home improvement, and farm supply stores.

Urban-country is about taking traditional country spaces and revamping them for a blended, modern look. The marriage of these two styles is the perfect recipe for a room that is all about function and good design.

REMEMBER COMMERCIAL CONCEPTS

If you are furnishing a new home, or restyling what you already have, try to connect urban and industrial objects and materials with country materials or furnishings. Just because a design solution works in an office, hospital, or other commercial setting, like a restaurant, it does not mean it can't be just as pleasing, or even more so, in your own home.

Integrating materials is an important part of that balance. Rubber treads and galvanized plumber's pipe makes for a durable, industrial staircase, which is supremely functional yet interestingly different when paired with warm wood flooring. Think about how rolling metal carts carry medicines throughout hospitals . . . and how handy one would be ferrying your child's toys between her bedroom and the living room. Think about how open stainless shelves used in commercial restaurant kitchens keep items immediately within reach. Costwise, they're

right: Urban-country style kitchens can be high, low, or midrange when it comes to prices and bells and whistles. It's not the money that counts—it's about the design and function. Here, a classic layout includes a stainless stove and concrete countertops beneath massive beams. Designed by LOCUS Architecture.

comparable to upper cabinets, and stylewise, you'll have a lot of visual interest and easier accessibility if you use them in your kitchen. Be open to alternatives when you consider materials, whether outside or inside your home.

Be on the lookout for items and ideas that can translate from the commercial to the residential realm. And think integration when it comes to everything—from your furnishings to the materials used on your house to your floor plan. Exploring creative combinations is how you'll be able to achieve a personalized look that uniquely represents you. ▪

above: Interesting old chairs and smooth wood floors lend character and a sense of uniqueness to this smart black-and-white kitchen. Note some other important elements of urban-country style here, too: the uncluttered countertop, the abundance of elegant, plain white serving dishes, and the choice of simple stemware.

right: A platform bed with simple linens creates a restful spot in this cozy bedroom, which includes a lamp created from an old surveyor's tool. Look for old objects that could be easily wired to create unusual lamps.

INTEGRATED—WHAT REALLY MATTERS

- If you're combining a household, have an honest discussion with your partner about what old pieces of furniture or items mean to you. For your family antiques, consider creating a list that explains the history behind the objects. The list will remind you and inform your future heirs about the circumstances behind the piece, much like labeling photographs. It's especially important to record family stories or memories about furnishings and objects if you give them away or bequeath them to other family members. Unless you communicate, your daughter, for instance, won't know that her great-grandparents bought one piece of furniture during the Depression, and that item is now her kitchen table.
- Think compromise, not confrontation, if you're combining a household.
- Always balance old and new in your rooms, and include different heights (of furnishings and lamps) and materials (woods, metals, and fabrics).
- When integrating different pieces, consider their visual appeal in your room. Think about textures.

facing: An urban-looking chair is right at home among upholstered pieces in this calming, sophisticated living room designed by Vicente Wolf. A trio of mirrors hung horizontally provides interest on the large wall, while the multitude of creamy hues makes for a restful and functional room.

left: Plumbing pipe and corrugated metal create a smart, unexpected breakfast bar and provide a nice contrast to the original brick wall.

facing: High style doesn't have to be expensive. The contrast between the curvy, easy-to-clean, plastic chairs (found on clearance) and a painted table that came from an unfinished furniture store provides a nice mix of urban/modern and simple elements. A $30 halogen ceiling-mounted light fixture from Ikea pivots to illuminate the table and the artwork, which was painted by the homeowner and hung without a frame.

old

U rban-country celebrates the blend of old and new, antique and contemporary, and of course, urban and rural. And that's precisely why having old things—whether from your family or not, whether truly antique or just plain old—is a critical component of the style.

facing: New York-based interior designer, author, and photographer Vicente Wolf displays a collection of shovels on a recessed ledge against a creamy-white background so that the individual pieces can be appreciated for their graphic quality as well as their patina.

WHY OLD ITEMS MATTER IN URBAN-COUNTRY HOMES

Older items in our homes connect us with our families, our past, and history. Old items often survive because of their high quality and fine workmanship, which alone is worth celebrating, and old objects lend a familiar sense of warmth to our homes. In an increasingly hectic world full of technology, stress, and noise, the simplicity of a handsome old table, an antique sideboard, or a hand-thrown piece of pottery can make us slow down and appreciate all that we have. It's also a way to connect the urban or suburban existence most of us live with the simpler country lifestyle of our dreams.

Old doesn't necessarily have to mean antique. The accepted industry standard of "antique" is an object that is 100 years old or older. You may have antiques in your family, or you may simply have old things that have been handed down by relatives. You may have stumbled across your prized piece at a yard sale or antique mall. It does not matter. What matters is that the items have meaning, you enjoy having them near you, and they serve a function.

GETTING THE LOOK

Incorporating "old" into your urban-country style home can mean contacting a millwork company and commissioning them to create a piece of furniture with a country feel but in a specific wood or finish of your choice. Some vintage farm tables can be slightly

SAVVY URBAN-COUNTRY STYLE TIP:
REPAIR, REUSE, OR RECYCLE.

Don't get into the trap of buying something wonderful that "needs some work," and then never working on it. Having a lot of broken items around can be overwhelming, not to mention the fact that they can take over your garage, basement, or attic. Reclaim your storage and recycle these needy pieces by giving them to someone who has the time, ability, and desire to fix them and use them. Be realistic about what you buy. A simple coat of paint or new upholstery is far more feasible than completely reworking and reinforcing a piece of furniture. The possession of a glue gun and finish nails doesn't qualify you (nor us!) to take on a big chair that needs to be completely reworked. A $10 piece of furniture is no bargain if it takes $300 to fix, and it's only worth it if you absolutely love it.

facing: A beautiful wood console serves as a fantastic foil for a modern sink and faucet in a home designed by New York-based Vicente Wolf.

facing: Feel free to have
fun with vintage pieces.
In this bathroom, an old
claw-foot tub was juiced
up with orange paint for a
more contemporary feel.

above: An antique dry sink—a classic country piece—
is used here as a base for a thoroughly urban sink and
faucet. More contrast is found between the simple,
contemporary shower surround and the clapboard
walls. A pine door, functional hooks, modern light
fixtures, and an old chair complete the look. Designed
by Looney Ricks Kiss.

lower or narrower than what we need for our modern lifestyle, so designing a new one in an ideal size modeled on an old piece can be an excellent solution. Likewise, salvaged boards can be planed into custom tables, tabletops, or benches, or can even be used to adorn walls or ceilings.

BUILDING OR REMODELING?

You can update older homes for today with new additions. Even the judicious removal of a wall can create a more open floor plan. The extent of your remodeling or building certainly depends on your own budget and interest, but some of the most vibrant homes are older houses where inherited problems have been solved with innovative materials and creative solutions. Many older homes have a wonderful uniqueness to them, a wealth of details, and are often composed of top-quality materials, so they are worth celebrating and saving. If you're up to the challenge, you can recycle a vintage home and bring it back online, so to speak.

If you are building or furnishing an urban-country home, a visit to your local salvage yard instead of your neighborhood building center can offer authentic vintage alternatives to new reproductions. Vintage sinks and tubs can be reglazed and incorporated into a contemporary design. If you choose this option, be sure you take measurements of the holes for faucets, drains, and spouts. If the sink or tub's hardware is missing, you'll have to purchase replacements that fit, and that can sometimes pose a challenge.

SAVVY URBAN-COUNTRY STYLE TIP: SEEK "INDUSTRIAL ANTIQUES."

As factories continue to close or update their equipment, an interesting array of salvaged carts, casters, and containers has entered the market. These historic, usually twentieth-century pieces are perfect partners for the urban-country look because they are usually supremely functional, yet wear decades of patina and use. If your town doesn't have an architectural salvage company, consider calling a demolition firm, local manufacturing plants, universities, or factories and asking if they have any surplus items for sale or if they ever hold sales. They may even be happy to give items to you for free. Likewise, see the resource section beginning on page 149 for some national companies that sell pieces online and will ship to you. Industrial relics can also be fabricated into functional pieces of furniture that will always be conversation pieces.

facing: Look for vintage locker bins at flea markets, yard sales, and online, or seek some of the very attractive reproductions on the market.

left: Cotton ticking invigorates this mahogany sofa, whose curves are offset by a smart, urban-looking steel and stained-oak coffee table. The pillows are more than decoration—the fabric on the middle cushion once hung as curtains in the homeowner's grandmother's home.

facing: Megan and Tim Johnson's serene, clutter-free master bath features wide-plank pine floors, a honed black granite countertop with under-mounted sinks, and a re-glazed tub that was discovered in a Nashville-area salvage yard. Note the trio of simple, galvanized lights that supplement recessed ceiling fixtures. Architecture by Kevin Coffey, Burke-Coffey Architects. Cabinetry by Schumacher's Custom Woodworking.

SAVVY URBAN-COUNTRY STYLE TIP:
STAGE YOUR COLLECTIBLES

The common adage of "display like things together" is a time-tested tip. A row of twentieth-century miners' lamps, a collection of clocks, a lineup of creamers—they all look best in a row next to each other. The key is to have an emotional attachment or personai reason to have your collection . . . don't just purchase to fill space.

facing: In the Johnsons' guest bath, an old sink found at a salvage yard provides an interesting focal point when paired with a new faucet. It also provides plenty of space for guests to keep toiletries. Just because a fixture was a kitchen sink in its past doesn't mean it has to always be a kitchen sink!

right: A re-glazed finish and a classic gooseneck faucet invigorate this claw-foot tub, which was found at a building salvage yard near Nashville. It can be challenging to find faucets for vintage sinks and tubs, so be sure you research the possibilities and take a tape measure with you when you visit an architectural salvage yard to measure the "spread," or the distance between the holes. Another option is to re-plate old metal hardware so that it looks new.

Old doors make interesting focal points when hung on sliding tracks. Old can also mean using lovely vintage Wedgwood dishes atop a contemporary table, or lining up vintage ironstone on open shelving in a kitchen.

The celebration of the blended aesthetic of old and new can also apply when it comes to the architecture of your home. Many of us live in older homes, and whether from the 1960s or the 1860s, these houses exude style from another era. It's important to remember, however, that just because you have a Victorian-era house, you don't have to embrace Victorian as your decorating style unless you want to. And since you picked up this book and are reading these words, chances are you probably don't want anything with button tufting or heavy brocade fabric in your home. But remember—opposites can be very attractive.

Use your imagination and work with what you have or with interesting things you find. Old furnishings or materials are indispensable elements of urban-country style, so choose your history carefully. ▪

OLD—WHAT REALLY MATTERS

- An urban-country home isn't complete without a country piece that references history, family, or fine workmanship. It can be high-style, sophisticated country or the most primitive of pieces, but it's a vital connection with the past.
- Try to educate yourself on furniture handed down through the family, and find out how it was used throughout the years. You will feel more connected to it and will have better stories.
- Be careful with old painted pieces, especially if you have young children or pets. Beautiful wood finishes (from pine to oak to mahogany) not only fit the urban-country style look better because they are simpler and more elegant, they are also a safer alternative than pieces coated with flaking lead paint. To learn more about lead paint, its potential hazards, and how to properly deal with it, please visit www.epa.gov/lead.
- If you can't find the object you're looking for, consider having it built.

facing: A contemporary slipcovered chair doubles as a dining chair and a spot to read near this vintage bookcase, which commands a corner of the Roddicks' dining room.

right: Retro-shaped sofas form a comfortable perch near the contemporary-style fireplace in this home, which doesn't include a mantel. Sometimes just covering a vintage piece with a wonderful solid color or ticking stripe can create an entirely fresh look for a tired old piece of furniture.

new

New is hip, hot, and now, so it's no surprise that a big part of urban-country style is capturing that awareness and energy and applying it to the home. Urban-country homes celebrate excellence in design, and particularly contemporary design, whether it is applied to an appliance, fabric, or building material. Also, since technology is a key component of our lives, we believe it should naturally be a key component in our decorating.

facing: Stock cabinetry from Ikea was used as the base for the Roddicks' kitchen in Nashville. Painted a warm gray and paired with clear resin pulls, the cabinets evoke an old-fashioned feel with a very up-to-date look. The glass tiles on the backsplash were stacked in an untraditional vertical pattern.

left: A metal flue reminiscent of a stovepipe unexpectedly eases out of the fireplace wall in this California house designed by Gray Matter Architecture.

above, right: Opposites attract: A slim, urban-looking metal stair rail is capped by small blocks of wood and provides a great contrast with blond wood stairs.

facing: Nowadays, retro style can come with a warranty. A smart citron refrigerator from Smeg provides a shot of color in this tiny kitchen, which features plenty of open shelving and metal and wood work surfaces.

EVERYTHING OLD IS NEW AGAIN

Today, old looks are reappearing in the sleekest of new packages, and we're all falling for them. If you love vintage stoves, today you can find a brand-new one that may look old but comes with a warranty and all the latest bells and whistles. Want a painted clapboard look for your new farmhouse? Fiber-cement shingles withstand the elements longer than wood and hold paint better, too. Desire an indestructible fabric for the furniture in your child's playroom? Today you can buy solution-dyed acrylic outdoor fabrics in a breathtaking array of colors, patterns, and even textures. New items can invigorate a room, just like new technology can invigorate our routines, save us time, and make life more entertaining.

Urban-country style uses these new products and technologies, which are critical to the way we live, while at the same time juxtaposing them with what you may already own, may have inherited, or may have picked up years ago at a yard sale. Urban-country style is not about starting over and adopting a new style, but rather about looking at your style as an organic process—something that is different for everyone, takes time, and grows with you.

INTRODUCING NEW ITEMS INTO YOUR SPACE

A critical component of urban-country is contemporary. And that means new furnishings (whether bought on a budget at a

left: In this corridor, note how the use of sliding overhead tracks makes the most of the space. Warm neutral colors lend a sophisticated feel, and a leather pull on the door in the foreground looks smart and feels good to the touch. Designed by Alchemy Architects.

facing: In this compact, urban-country kitchen designed by Nancy Gent, open stainless shelving, sleek appliances, chocolate rubber floors, and Corian countertops provide urban energy, while the solid maple cabinetry, simple pulls and wall-mounted faucet feel familiar and are completely integrated into the design. Renovations by Scooter J. Construction, Nashville.

facing and above: While the new kitchen in this Texas house is clearly contemporary, its generous use of open shelving, its functionality, and its simplicity make it worthy of study.

discount store or bought online from Italy) and fresh accessories to complement your evolving style and to add dialogue to the wonderful old items in your home. Perhaps you'll want to pair a new cocktail table in front of your old sofa, get some new chairs for the family dining table, or perhaps introduce some fantastic new lighting. You'll probably want to get a new bed, and definitely a new mattress.

Why not pair fabulous molded resin chairs in vivid aqua with that elegant old secretary desk? Why not consider those brushed-aluminum lamps with the drum shades that you have had your eye on for months for the vintage sideboard in your dining room? Mixing urban and country elements gives you a collected look that is familiar, of-the-moment, and one-of-a-kind. By nature, your home won't look completely store-bought, although many individual pieces may come from your favorite catalog or store.

above: In the Roddicks' home in Nashville, a single strand of picture wire and wooden clothespins make a wonderful, inexpensive system for hanging an ever-changing art collection.

above: When a house has wonderful architectural detailing, such as the panels seen here, urban-style furnishings can provide a fabulous foil.

Think about how your technology—your TV, DVD player, stereo, MP3 player—fits into your lifestyle. Take the most popular piece of technology most of us have—the television. What is the urban-country style approach? It's time to rethink the armoire. There is nothing wrong with having your TV on a smart, stylish cart in your living room. The Europeans have been doing it for years, and more than one good-natured laugh has been had at the American craze for armoires and cabinets to cover up all things techno in our homes. While some urban-country style homes will use a country piece as a cover-up for the flat screen, others will simply put the flat screen atop an old chest of drawers and use those drawers to store DVDs. The choice is up to you.

It's important to pay attention to how entertainment technology is also morphing into our appliances, such as the new refrigerators with built-in TV screens. But if the latter isn't

facing: Open shelving below the vanities in this master bath designed and built by homeowner Andy Roddick store everyday essentials. The Roddicks chose to paint their walls and trim the same tone for a more contemporary look in their Victorian-era home.

this page: A contemporary sink and integrated counter is the modern equivalent of a big, one-piece country farm sink with drain boards. The large mirror and slim, modern light fixtures set off the room, which includes a row of functional hooks on the opposite wall and a modern version of the traditional gooseneck faucet.

on your to-buy list, consider a commercial product, the wall-mounted bracket that holds your TV up near the ceiling, as a solution. If you're purchasing one of the newer, flat-screen televisions, you might want to consider a long sideboard to hold the TV and also provide storage space for the attendant media, such as CDs and DVDs. When flanked by two tall, narrow buffet lamps, this arrangement can be very pleasing.

In terms of media storage, consider new alternatives, from a piece of ready-made furniture to a custom solution or even a horizontal slice of "captured" space between wall studs to create a sinuous open shelf.

It is important to be discerning when you buy new pieces of furniture or accessories. Look for things that will work with what you have and will complement your house. For example, when seeking a contemporary chair, make sure you start by measuring the height of your old desk. Also, price and design excellence are often not connected; there are a lot of low-cost things, from side tables to lamps, that look terrific yet won't break the bank.

left: If you're lucky enough to be building a new kitchen, build in more storage than you need. Here, the Roddicks used a vertical slice of shelving to create extra display space for country-style pitchers.

facing: In the Roddicks' dining room, a salvaged tabletop is paired with a contemporary-style base made from chunky wooden blocks. Inexpensive cotton slipcovers (these are from Target) transform basic chairs into stylish seating.

KEEP IT COUNTRY

The key is to keep things clean and crisp, yet still country. Strive for balance when you combine old and new, country and urban. When choosing new furniture or fabrics, keep simplicity in mind and gravitate toward simple silhouettes, solids, and graphic stripes. In general, look for fabrics that are simple, like ticking; avoid overly luxe materials like mohair. New pieces should not fight with antiques—you will find that the new actually enhances the old. That is why it is important to choose older pieces that look good on their own and can hold their own when paired with something new. An example would be a piece with a sophisticated shape and created from an interesting material, or something that merely catches the eye. Look for uniqueness. Good design is not restricted to a single decade, country, or century. The main point to remember is that when you buy a new piece of furniture or an accessory, purchase something with style *and* quality.

facing: Ideas that work well inside also work well outside your home. Here, Janus et Cie's Cannes chairs are pulled around three separate tables to create a larger outdoor dining area on this covered porch. If you have a large outdoor area to furnish, consider purchasing the same tables and chairs so that you can create one big table if needed.

above: Natural materials and colors form a tasteful tablesetting that transitions from day to evening with ease.

this page, left: The Ian Mankin store in London, England is a premier destination for anyone seeking cotton ticking. The shop specializes in 100% cotton fabrics in a range of colors, stripes, and checks.

this page, right: A simple galvanized container from a farm supply store is a great spot in which to store extra bedding.

facing, top: The Martin family's country-inspired kitchen, designed by Nashville based firm DA/AD, features soapstone counters and sports urban appeal thanks to its commercial restaurant-style faucet, which pulls out to become a sprayer. The brown leather bar stools are not only comfortable, but their washable surface means sticky little fingerprints quickly disappear. There is no need for a window treatment: not only are these traditional windows lovely to look at in their own right, but they also overlook a peaceful Tennessee field.

facing, bottom: If you're building or remodeling, specify that your cabinets be designed to reach the ceiling—you'll be glad about the extra storage. Designed by LOCUS Architecture.

SAVVY URBAN-COUNTRY STYLE TIP: *COTTON TICKING + OLD FURNISHINGS = A FRESH, URBAN-COUNTRY LOOK.*

Cotton ticking comes in a variety of colors and stripes and injects instant appeal when applied to an old piece of furniture or used as slipcover over an otherwise ugly upholstered cube. Ticking is generally affordable, soft, easy to clean, and is readily available at almost any fabric store (although we've found that some of the world's best examples are from Ian Mankin, a British company—see the Resources section on page 149). Best of all, it's inviting. When ticking is used to upholster a formal piece of furniture, such as a chair or sofa with graceful lines, it instantly adds a sense of casual style.

THE URBAN-COUNTRY STYLE LIFE

Urban-country is more than a style. It's a philosophy, too. It's not about buying everything from a store, impressing your family or friends, making your life (or cleaning routine) more difficult than it has to be, or consuming more than you need. It's sensible, sustainable style, and a look that is focused on the real-life performance of your life. It's function that's also beautiful, unexpected, simple, and a combination of old and new—elements that work together to become an integrated look.

Urban-country style works on the guidelines of FUSION: functional, unexpected, simple, integrated, old, and new. The only other guideline should be your wallet and your heart. After all, it is for you and for the little bit of urban and little bit of country you have inside.

above: This functional kitchen connects urban ideas, like translucent panels used for the base cabinets, with simple country elements such as open shelving, an uncomplicated layout, and plenty of natural light.

facing: This urban-country style house designed by LOCUS Architecture incorporates a window pattern that references older homes. While clearly contemporary, it melds metal with country materials such as wood and stone.

left: Another version of sliding doors on overhead tracks helps connect the indoors with the garden in this open-plan home designed by Gray Matter Architecture. The visible floor joists from the second level are reminiscent of barn ceilings.

facing: Urban-country style is clearly casual, but the living room of this California house also shows how sophisticated the style can be and how open rooms can convey the feeling of being in a big loft—either in a city or in a country barn.

facing: Nancy Gent worked with Jim Mylcraine to design a custom white oak table with a plank top and ebony stain for the Murphy family's dining room in Nashville. A large canvas painted the same color as the wall provides a space for family and friends to contribute inspirational words. Keeping the words on canvas rather than on the bare wall means that the ever-morphing artwork can be moved at a later date.

this page, top: This stretched canvas, adorned with messages from family and friends, provides both a keepsake and a piece of art in one item, and provides an unmistakable focal point on a large wall in the Murphy family's dining room.

this page, bottom left: Don't clutter your tabletops with superfluous items. Simple, seeded glass hurricane shades (these are from Pizitz in Florida) filled with sand and basic white pillars provide an elegant counterpoint to the dark tabletop.

this page, bottom right: Smart khaki and black ticking from London-based Ian Mankin lends a country feel to the sophisticated shape of the black wicker chairs in the Murphys' dining room.

this page, top and bottom: Stroll down the aisles of your local building supply store to glean ideas for furniture, closet components, or shelving that can be created from metal pipes and fittings.

facing: Nancy Gent worked with Dan Crosby to create this urban-style pipe bed, which is perfectly at home in a teen's room. Quilted cotton bedding in bold colors from Utility Canvas continues the city theme.

NEW—WHAT REALLY MATTERS

- Save up for primary new pieces like mattresses and sofas, rather than going into debt to buy cheap options.
- Look for stylish ways to display your technology. Everything doesn't have to be hidden.
- Consider commercial alternatives when it comes to windows, doors, hardware, carpets, and fabrics. You'll find a more contemporary range of styles, yet the prices will still typically be less than if you commissioned custom designs.

this page, left: Reproduction metal chairs have been used in commercial, military, and medical settings for years, and now they provide a fresh look in homes. They're also ultra-durable, lightweight, and easy-to-clean—a big plus for families with small children.

this page, right: The easy on-off metal toggle switch is a stock item at The Home Depot.

facing: In the Murphy house, which is a renovated ranch, a stone fireplace is set off with streamlined hurricane shades, a slipcovered cube, and an architectural lamp for interest. Keeping artwork, such as this black-and-white portrait, in an unadorned frame provides balance.

resources

Many wonderful resources may be hidden gems near where you live. Look for antique stores, flea markets, metal fabricators, auto body shops, restaurant supply stores, unfinished furniture stores, and plastic fabricators in your area. You can always show pictures to local artisans and have them re-create furnishings or accessories to fit your needs.

facing: Another bed design by Nancy Gent and built by Jim Mylcraine is perfect for a small space since it includes an integrated light fixture with a headboard-mounted switch. Accessibility to the light switch from the headboard is a safer and easier option than fumbling for a switch on a nearby lamp.

ARCHITECTS, BUILDERS, AND DESIGNERS

Alchemy Architects
856 Raymond Ave.
St. Paul, MN 55114
Tel: 651.647.6650
www.alchemyarchitects.com

Burke Coffey Architecture Design Inc.
Kevin Coffey and Don Burke, principals
230 Franklin Rd., Ste. 817
Franklin, TN 37064
Tel: 615.599.2557
Fax: 615.599.2933
kevinbcad@bellsouth.net

DA/AD Architecture
2520 White Ave.
Nashville, TN 37204
Tel: 615.248.3223
www.daad-group.com
Project team for Martin residence:
John Abernathy, AIA; Nick Dryden, AIA;
Susannah Petrounov; Kim Martin

DuCharme Architecture
7745 Herschel Ave.
La Jolla, CA 92037
Tel: 858.454.5205
www.ducharmearch.com

Nancy Gent Design
Interior Design
Tel: 615.804.9923

Gray Matter Architecture
639 E. Channel Rd.
Santa Monica, CA 90402
Tel: 310.454.7960
www.graymatterarchitecture.com

Beth Haley Design
Interior Design
Beth Haley, Allied ASID
937 Woodland St.
Nashville, TN 37206
Tel: 615.228.3664
Fax: 615.228.3194
www.bethhaleydesign.com

Kennon | Taylor Architects, PLLC
Matthew K. Taylor, AIA
1130 Eighth Ave. South
Nashville, TN 37203
Tel: 615.250.8150
www.kennon-taylor.com

Lake | Flato
Architecture
311 Third St., Ste. 200
San Antonio, TX 78205
Tel: 210.227.3335
www.lakeflato.com

LOCUS Architecture, Ltd.
1500 Jackson St. NE, Ste. 333
Minneapolis, MN 55413
Tel: 612.706.5600
www.locusarchitecture.com

Looney Ricks Kiss Architects
Architecture and Planning
175 Toyota Plaza, Ste. 600
Memphis, TN 38103
Tel: 901.521.1440
www.lrk.com

Scooter J. Construction
Custom Builder
1022 Walnut Ct.
Goodlettsville, TN 37072
Tel: 615.414.4463

Vicente Wolf Associates, Inc.
Interior Design
333 W. Thirty-ninth St.
New York, NY 10018
Tel: 212.465.0590
www.vicentewolfassociates.com

SHOPS

Area Home
www.areahome.com
Contemporary bedding

Boltz
www.boltz.com
Metal furniture

Diamond Foam & Fabric
611 South La Brea
Los Angeles, CA 90036
Tel: 323.931.8148
Swatches available

Herndon & Merry/Garden Park Antiques
7121 Cockrill Bend Blvd.
Nashville, TN 37209
Tel: 615.350.6655
www.gardenpark.com
Custom furnishings and industrial and garden antiques

Ian Mankin Ltd.
109 Regent's Park Rd.
Primrose Hill
London NW1 8UR
United Kingdom
0044.20.7722.0997
www.ianmankin.com
Our favorite source for cotton ticking. Swatches available. Mail-order for U.S. customers via phone.

IKEA
www.ikea.com
Urban and country-inspired furniture and accessories

The Iron Gate
338 Main St.
Franklin, TN 37064
615.791.7511
Full-service interior design, unusual antiques, gifts, and fabrics

Mitchell Gold + Bob Williams
www.mgandbw.com
A favorite source for upholstered furniture and accessories

Nouveau Classics of Nashville
3201 Belmont Blvd.
Nashville, TN 32712
Tel: 615.383.3164
Urban-inspired furniture and accessories

Pizitz Home & Cottage
PO Box 4670
Seaside, FL 32459
Tel: 850.231.2240
Beach-inspired furnishings, accessories, and gifts

Pottery Barn
www.potterybarn.com
Country-inspired furniture and accessories

Scarlett Scales Antiques
212 S. Margin St.
Franklin, TN 37064
Tel: 615.791.4097 or 615.390.5231
www.scarlettscales.com
European linens, unusual country and urban antiques, and full-service interior design

Utility Canvas
PO Box 217
Gardner, NY 12525
Tel: 800.680.9290
www.utilitycanvas.com
Quilted bedding and home accessories

SUPPLIERS/MANUFACTURERS

Curtain Fair
Tel: 800.497.1588
www.curtainfair.com
Ceiling-mounted shower curtain tracks

Farmers Cooperative Association, Inc.
www.farmerscoop.com
*Farm and garden supplies, galvanized
containers, and stock tanks*

The Home Depot
www.homedepot.com
*Building supplies, lighting, plumbing,
and metal accessories*

Janus et Cie
www.janusetcie.com
Indoor/outdoor wicker and other furnishings

Lowe's
www.lowes.com
*Building supplies, lighting, plumbing,
and metal accessories*

Martha Campbell, The Alternative
13056 Hwy. 23
Vina, AL 35593
Tel: 256.356.8280
Custom upholstery, cushions, and drapery

Myers Truck and Caster Sales Company
746 Douglas Ave.
PO Box 60175
Nashville, TN 37206
Tel: 800.321.6732
www.myerstruck.com
Casters

Jim Mylcraine
1006 Lakeside Drive
Ashland, TN 37015
Tel: 615.207.3432
Furniture

Tractor Supply Company
www.mytscstore.com
*Farm and garden supplies, galvanized
containers, and stock tanks*

Viking Range
www.vikingrange.com
*Commercial-grade stoves and kitchen
supplies*

Vintage Millworks Inc.
525 Merrit Ave.
Nashville, TN 37203
Tel: 615.244.8044
www.vintage-millworks.com
Custom cabinetry and millwork

PHOTOGRAPHERS

Chris Little Photography
8343 Roswell Rd. #132
Atlanta, GA 30350
Tel: 770.641.9688
www.chrislittlephotography.com

Scott Lowden Photography
634 North Highland Ave., Loft A
Atlanta, GA 30306
Tel: 404.873.6768
www.scottlowden.com

Sanford Myers
Sanford Photography
www.sanfordmyers.com
Tel: 615.330.6742

photography credits

facing: The concept of a cozy chair by the fireplace takes an urban-country turn with a cowhide-covered club chair and a modern firebox. It's an unexpected combination of new elements, but one that works because the traditional lines of the chair complement the urban-looking fireplace. Note how the simple metal container holds firewood ... and it also contains dirt and splinters better than the expected basket.

COURTESY OF ALCHEMY ARCHITECTS
24, 38, 43, 60, 76, 87, 122 (right), 124, 131

BRADY ARCHITECTURAL PHOTOGRAPHY
30, 39, 71, 82–83

CHRIS LITTLE PHOTOGRAPHY
42, 56

JONN COOLIDGE
46 (bottom)

GREY CRAWFORD, COURTESY OF GRAY MATTER ARCHITECTURE
16, 54 (both), 86, 93, 122 (left), 140, 141

RETO GUNTLI/ ZAPAIMAGES.COM
2, 8, 20, 23, 41, 43 (right), 46 (top left, top right), 74, 101, 110, 119, 123

BRUNO HELBLING/ ZAPAIMAGES.COM
26, 100

HESTER + HARDAWAY PHOTOGRAPHERS
40

ELIZABETH BETTS HICKMAN
50, 91, 104, 115, 116, 117

JOHN L. HICKMAN
49, 52, 57

COURTESY OF IAN MANKIN
LTD.
136 (left)

COURTESY OF JANUS ET CIE
6, 15, 19, 61, 69, 72, 134

BILL LAFEVOR, COURTESY
OF KENNON TAYLOR
ARCHITECTS P.L.L.C.
53

COURTESY OF LAKE|FLATO
ARCHITECTS
62, 94

COURTESY OF LOCUS
ARCHITECTURE, LTD.
32, 33, 55 (left)

GAIL OWENS
78, 79, 84–85

ROBERT MEIER
55 (right), 92

SANFORD MYERS,
SANFORD PHOTOGRAPHY
22 (both), 36, 48, 58, 64 (top right, bottom), 65, 73, 85, 88, 89, 105, 113, 114, 118, 120, 125, 128, 129, 130, 132, 133, 135, 136 (right), 137 (top), 142, 143 (all), 144 (both), 145, 146 (both), 147, 148

CLAUDIO SANTINI,
COURTESY OF GRAY MATTER
ARCHITECTURE
70